SUPERFOOD SANDWICHES

Crafting Nutritious Sandwiches with Superfoods for Every Meal and Occasion

Katie Chudy
founder of the Small Boston Kitchen

Fair Winds Press
100 Cummings Center, Suite 406L
Beverly, MA 01915

fairwindspress.com • quarryspoon.com

First published in the USA in 2015 by
Fair Winds Press, a member of
Quarto Publishing Group USA Inc.
100 Cummings Center
Suite 406-L
Beverly, MA 01915-6101
www.fairwindspress.com
Visit www.QuarrySPOON.com and help us celebrate food and culture one
spoonful at a time!

19 18 17 16 15   1 2 3 4 5

ISBN: 978-1-59233-663-0

Digital edition published in 2015
eISBN: 978-1-62788-299-6
Library of Congress Cataloging-in-Publication Data available

Cover and book design by *tabula rasa* graphic design
Photography by Katie Chudy

Printed and bound in China

The information in this book is for educational purposes only. It is not
intended to replace the advice of a physician or medical practitioner.
Please see your health care provider before beginning any new health
program.

For my husband, Richard. Your immense amounts of love, support, encouragement, and especially comic relief made doing all of this possible. I'm so lucky to be able to share this life with you.

Contents

Introduction

"Too few people understand a really good sandwich."

—*James Beard*

My love affair with sandwiches started early and with a simple introduction to a humble grilled cheese made by my mom, at our home in western Massachusetts. It was toasty on the outside and gave way to a molten, cheesy center. I found so much pleasure in the contrast of textures and playing with the strands of stretchy cheese. In that moment, I just remember feeling so happy and loved.

I was not always "into" food, though. I was an incredibly picky eater growing up and remained that way through college. My lunches were plain and simple: turkey on caraway-studded rye and with a healthy slathering of mustard and sometimes a thin slice of sharp provolone cheese. It was when I moved to northern Virginia that I started to experience food from different ethnicities and cultures. I was blown away by the intense flavors of rich curries and tried Thai food for the first time, falling in love with the likes of tom yum soup and pad ki mow. The more I tried, the more I was drawn to learning; I spent more and more time in the kitchen, playing around with new flavors and ingredients, making everything from scratch. I subscribed to every cooking magazine I could find, and my cookbook collection grew immensely. I couldn't get enough.

Around this time, I was introduced to different vegetables that my picky childhood ways kept me from trying. I was cooking sweet potatoes; had my first taste of delicate, oniony leeks; and learned the pleasure of pungently sharp, freshly grated horseradish. Meanwhile, I was learning about nutrition and how to care for myself better by incorporating more healthful ingredients into my lifestyle. Flaxseeds, packed with omega-3 fatty acids, found their way into my yogurt and the breads that I couldn't seem to stop making. These nutritionally whole ingredients have a name superfoods. I found that the more I added them into my diet, the healthier I felt, the less I got sick, and the more energy I had. Since then, I've continued to include as many superfoods as I can into my daily life.

When I finally moved back to Massachusetts, my small studio apartment offered only a galley kitchen with a simple stove and counter space the size of an encyclopedia, but I was cooking more than ever before. At the time, I was working a corporate job and increasingly feeling dissatisfied with my career path. I felt that I wanted to be as happy with my day-to-day job as I felt when I was in the kitchen. I started a blog, the Small Boston Kitchen, in 2009 to help me record the recipes that I was creating. I started to explore working professionally with food but couldn't figure out how to make the numbers work. In December 2010, longing for more structure to my cooking, I applied to the Cambridge School of Culinary Arts, in Massachusetts. Upon acceptance,

I quit my job to focus on trying to make a career in food. At that time I met Richard, a local personal chef, and started shadowing him and then began working alongside him at catering jobs. Hitting it off, we decided to join forces and start our own personal chef and catering company, right around the same time that we started dating.

Our company is called the Skinny Beet, named after the combination of our Polish last names; Richard's last name means "skinny" and mine means "beet soup." We started with a few clients and worked long hours, doing all we could do to get work and network in Boston. We had little money and spent any that we had on groceries to practice our skills and develop our arsenal of recipes. Wanting to be as efficient and frugal as possible, we started living off of sandwiches. They were substantial enough to fill up on, and they helped us make great use of leftovers and stretch ingredients. They were also an easy way to incorporate lots of superfoods into our diet and eat healthfully when we didn't have much time or money to spare.

Within a year's time, our company had taken off, and we had plenty of clients to cook for. As our lives became full of working and cooking, we continued to turn to sandwiches to fit our hunger needs. They were easy to assemble and satisfying to eat at all hours. Washed down with a cold beer or a post-work glass of wine, sandwiches became a celebratory symbol of a successful day and of a happy life, doing what I loved most with those I loved.

These days, with gluten-free, Paleo, bread-hating trends soaring, the sandwich gets a bad rap. Some people argue the sandwich is classless and boring, a poor dietary choice. But it doesn't have to be that way! Using recognized superfoods, fresh vegetables, fruits, cheeses, meats (and we're not talking about supermarket deli meats here), and good-quality, freshly baked breads makes any sandwich a very respectable and versatile meal. A sandwich is an excellent way to effectively use leftovers, creating a

budget- and family-friendly way to enjoy a meal. In a more sophisticated sense, everything can be made from scratch—from the bread to the condiments and everything in between. This book provides tips and shortcuts for people in a hurry as well as more detailed recipes and options, making some extra effort in the kitchen well worth it.

Many of us are on the go constantly, yet we value our nutrition and pay close attention to our health and food choices. Sandwiches can help us maintain a healthy lifestyle, featuring a wide variety of healthy proteins, vegetables, and fruits in a cost-effective way. In this book, I share with you my passion for sandwiches and the techniques that I have learned as a professionally trained chef.

This book is meant to revitalize the concept of the everyday sandwich, drawing on global flavors and incorporating healthy superfoods that people know they should be eating but often struggle to incorporate into their meals and diets. With a range of recipes, from simple to more complex, this book celebrates the sandwich—a hearty meal option that is nutritious enough for any time of the day or night—while featuring fun and quirky recipes that will liven up your kitchen.

HOW TO USE THIS BOOK

I hate the word *diet.* More specifically, I hate the notion that it's a dramatic, sufferable change that we make in what we eat for the sake of trying to slim down. It's usually a painful process of eliminating foods deemed "bad," and it often precedes a specific event, such as swimsuit season, or more specifically, a high school reunion or wedding. But once said season or event is over, it's back to eating the way we used to, which leads to gaining the weight back and sometimes even more, which cues back up the start of the suffering, vicious cycle. I've had a fling with most diets. Fat was the enemy in the 1990s, and I remember naively eating only foods with the magic words *fat free* emblazoned on their packages. Then, in the early 2000s, carbs were the enemy. So I navigated away from high-carb foods (or tried my best to). This one was the hardest for me; I missed my carbs, and the breakup with them was too much to bear. It was at that moment I decided I was done with diets forever and that I needed to learn more about how to properly feed myself and get the right nutrients, rather than following whatever diet was currently trending.

In my research, I found that I always gravitated toward a couple of basic concepts. They are to make my own food when I can so that I'll know exactly what's in it, and to take the time to make things that would excite my palate. This was the fun part. There's a whole world of flavors that I had yet to discover. I also learned that there were a lot of fruits and vegetables that I had never tried, not to mention the various ways of preparing them that can totally change the outcome of a meal.

It's my hope that the recipes in this book encourage you to think about sandwiches in a different way, and not just as a quick and easy lunchtime option. Some sandwiches in this book will satisfy the need for something fast and thrown together. Other recipes require more prep, more hands-on time, and a little more love, but I can promise you that the results will be well worth the time and effort, whether you're cooking for yourself, a significant other, an entire family, or a whole gang. This book will teach you new techniques, and I'll introduce you to new ingredients. I developed the recipes to suit my tastes, and I encourage you to tweak them so that they suit yours, too.

This book is broken down by category, starting with the very foundation—the bread. There are several superfood bread recipes that are used to make many of the sandwiches, and if you've never made your own bread at home, you're in for a treat. Not only will the aroma of freshly baked bread fill your home, but it also tastes much better than store-bought bread, and it's healthier. After the bread chapter, it's

on to superfood condiments before getting to the real focus of the book—the sandwiches themselves. Although most of the sandwiches contain several different superfoods, they are organized in sections based on their predominate superfood. Each recipe highlights the superfoods included so that they can be easily identified. For the fruit and vegetable definition sticklers out there, the categories are based on what is generally accepted to be a fruit and a vegetable. For example, cucumbers and zucchini are technically fruits; however, they are often labeled vegetables, so that's where they appear in this book.

PLEASE, DON'T CALL THIS A DIET BOOK

This book is not supposed to be a fast way to drop extra pounds. It's not supposed to be a quick fix, but it can be part of your lifestyle—by developing or maintaining the habit of incorporating superfoods into your daily diet in an approachable, fun, and creative way. There is fat in this book. There is meat, and there is cheese and gluten. The truth is that your body needs fat to keep you fueled; it is necessary for that feeling of satiety that will keep you from overeating.

The portions of these sandwiches may be smaller than standard sandwiches that you enjoy while dining out. It's been my experience that smaller, more satisfying portions help me stay within my ideal weight. Also, you can always omit foods if your hunger level isn't high and you're looking for something lighter, or you can add more, make them larger, or just eat two if the hunger monster is really striking.

These recipes also contain salt. If used properly, salt can seduce the flavors out of your food in ways that nothing else can, and seasoning food properly is the easiest way to change your cooking game and elevate things a bit. Because we are mostly working with ingredients in their raw and natural state, they need salt. Season while you cook to get the most flavor out of your ingredients. Taste regularly for seasoning and adjust accordingly to suit your tastes. My salt of choice is always kosher salt. I like that I can feel the big flakes between my fingers and that the salt crystals' flat surfaces cover more ground than regular table salt does. If you're not already using kosher salt, consider making the switch.

SOURCING INGREDIENTS

Taking the time to source good ingredients is one of the most important factors for nutritious results when cooking, and in this case, better sandwiches. If you start out with the best ingredients—and that doesn't always mean the most expensive—the results will be significantly better than beginning a recipe with mediocre ingredients. Start by learning what is currently in season. You can easily get information on what's in season in your area online. I like to use the seasonal ingredient map on www.epicurious.com. A quick search will bring it up. Of course, you can make things that aren't in season, but they tend to taste better when enjoyed during their natural season.

It's also a great practice to shop at a reputable grocery store, or even better, a farmers' market. If you aren't sure how to select an ingredient, you can always ask or just go with your instinct. I always smell the produce that I put into my cart. In most cases, especially with fruit, I find that if the aroma is fresh and it smells great, then it usually tastes great.

When it comes to sourcing meats and other proteins, always buy food that looks fresh. Typically a store that has a butcher counter and a fish counter is better than one that only sells prepack-aged meats and seafood from large companies. Hormones, additives, and preservatives have no place in proteins. Get comfortable with the fact that this method of selecting proteins may cost a little more. Personally, I'd rather eat the best-quality meat that I can and less of it than have a higher abundance of protein in my diet that isn't natural or contains ingredients that shouldn't be in there. Spending money on the best ingredients that I can buy is totally worth it to me.

GETTING STARTED

As with any cookbook, I encourage you to read through each recipe in its entirety before you start. Because this book is meant to introduce you to ingredients that you may not be familiar with or certain techniques that you may not know, the Internet is a great resource to get that information. Once you're comfortable with the recipe, its ingredients and techniques, it helps to lay out all of the ingredients, measured according to the recipe and ready to go. This practice is called *mise en place*, and it is great in helping you stay organized while cooking, not to mention that it sounds cool.

I created all of these recipes, and each one has been tested in my home and in other home kitchens, but each oven, stove, and kitchen is different. Because of that, there's a fair amount of intuition that goes along with cooking from a recipe and you have to trust your gut (pun intended). If something doesn't look or feel right, use your judgment to get the results that you want. Remember, certain factors such as atmosphere, altitude, humidity, and oven temperatures vary, so if your homemade bread is not cooked through after the amount of time that I specified, bake it a little longer and keep checking it. Always stay close to food that is cooking so you can keep an eye on it and address any problems that may occur (such as a pot boiling over or food burning in the oven).

This book is also meant to be a starting point for you, and it will hopefully inspire you to create your own superfood sandwiches. These recipes are meant to be flexible and interchangeable and give you lots of room to incorporate your own creativity. If that Roasted Strawberry Balsamic Steak Sauce sounds like it would be an incredible addition to your chicken sandwich instead, by all means, make a change. Feel free to add and subtract things based on your own personal tastes and dietary preferences. If you're vegan, just tailor recipes to your own needs by omitting any dairy and swapping proteins for a vegetarian option such as tofu or roasted eggplant. And if you happen to hate pecans but love almonds, swap them out. Pretty much all foods that are in the same family are interchangeable. For example, all citrus can be switched out in recipes, as can all nuts, most cheeses, and various vinegars. I encourage you to play around with different flavors or think of them as an easy way to just use up what you have on hand. Along the way, I will suggest substitutions.

Don't be afraid to make note of your progress right in the book, which is something I do with my cookbooks. I like to note things that I swapped out or tried differently so that next time I go to make the same thing, I'll remember what I liked and what I didn't. To me, the dirtier and more written in my cookbooks are, the more loved they are. But if defacing your book with scribbles isn't your style—and it's not for everyone—then sticky notes work well, too.

STOP THROWING AWAY LEFTOVERS
Every year for Thanksgiving, we make more than enough food so that we can have days of sandwiches stuffed with all the fixings—roasted turkey, cranberry sauce, and other odds and ends that sneak their way in, too. I've gotten into the habit of thinking ahead and keeping with this mentality all year-round, which saves me a lot of time and money. If I'm going to roast a chicken, I buy way more than I need for one night's dinner to make sure that I've got enough for leftovers. I know that if I have items in my refrigerator that are fresh and made by me, I can easily work these ingredients into sandwiches. That way, I'm less likely to want to get takeout or fall victim to a poor food choice. In a pinch, I find that all of these little items from yesterday's meal perfectly transform into delicious sandwiches.

A good part of the recipes in this book can be made from leftovers, and I encourage you to do so. You'll find that leftover rice finds its way easily into the veggie burgers and last night's extra roasted vegetables can be tonight's Sweet Potato "Falafel" Sandwich (page 104). If you don't already practice the art of thinking ahead and cooking extras, or if you feel that you don't utilize your leftovers and you have to toss them out, I hope that this book gives you inspiration. This will save you time and money, which everyone can appreciate.

ONE FINAL NOTE: RELAX AND HAVE FUN!
To really enjoy cooking and derive pleasure from it, relax, have fun, and just go with it. I've found through my own experiences in cooking that somewhere along the way things may change directions, or halfway through the process you'll get inspiration from something you haven't thought of before. Go with it. Learn and don't be afraid to end up with something a little different than what you had originally planned. That's when the act of cooking becomes immensely enjoyable. Take the time to get to know your ingredients, smelling and tasting them along the way. Even 10 minutes spent cooking can be quite rewarding and a relaxing experience and break from life's stressors. There's a huge personal payoff and sense of accomplishment at the end of preparing a meal that I've never been able to replicate elsewhere in life. Taking the time to create a meal, nourishing yourself and others, is a wonderful way to express love and tell someone that you care, even if that someone is just yourself. And with that, I invite you to enjoy using this book as much as I've enjoyed creating it.

Featured Superfoods

Before we dive headfirst into the delicious sandwiches, let's take a minute to learn a little about the nutrient-dense whole foods they contain. Following is a list of all of the superfoods that are included in this book and a little information about why they're so important for your diet. There are other foods in this book that may provide health benefits, but for the purposes of defining superfoods, this is the list we will use. It's based on research done by several dietary professionals who identify these foods as the healthiest and most beneficial. Also, for your ease, each recipe in this book identifies all of the superfoods in each sandwich.

Acai berries: Some studies show that acai berries are even more antioxidant-rich than cranberries and other berries. Antioxidants can help fight against heart disease and cancer, as well as keep eye diseases at bay and skin looking youthful.

Almonds: This is one of the most nutritionally dense nuts, providing lots of fiber, potassium, magnesium, calcium, vitamin E, and iron. It is a true superfood of the nut world.

Apples: Apples are associated with the reduced risk of certain cancers and cardiovascular diseases; they are an excellent source of fiber, too.

Arugula: Containing only 5 calories a cup, arugula is packed with vitamins A and K, which help your eyes and bones.

Avocados: Avocados contain monounsaturated fat, which helps lower bad cholesterol and has been linked to a reduced rate of heart disease, stroke, and cancer.

Bananas: Bananas are a good source of fiber and potassium, which can help you with blood pressure regulation.

Basil: Basil contains flavonoids, which have been known to fight cancer cells and prevent their growth.

Beans: Beans keep you full because of their high fiber and protein content. They are also high in resistant starch (RS), which is resistant to digestion, passing through the stomach to the colon. Most of the calories consumed from RS can't be absorbed.

Beets/beet greens: Beets contain betalains, which give them their purple hue. Studies suggest that fruits and vegetables high in betalains can help decrease your risk of cancer. Beets are also known to help strengthen vital organs.

Black garlic: Cooked slowly over several weeks until it develops a deep, rich, and slightly sweet taste, black garlic is soft and dark in color. Black garlic is rich in antioxidants.

Blackberries: This berry has more antioxidants than other common berries, such as strawberries, blueberries, and cranberries.

Blueberries: High in antioxidants as well as vitamin C, blueberries have anti-inflammatory properties and can help lower your risk of heart disease and cancer.

Broccoli: Packed with vitamin C and folate, broccoli also has a high concentration of vitamins and minerals as well as fiber. Eating broccoli may help reduce the risk of heart disease, cancer, and stroke.

Brown rice: Linked to reducing the risk of developing type 2 diabetes, brown rice has cholesterol-lowering properties and is high in fiber.

Brussels sprouts: This member of the cabbage family has been linked to promoting a healthy cardiovascular system and preventing certain types of cancer.

Buckwheat: A great source of fiber, protein, and calcium, buckwheat has also been shown to potentially slow the rate of glucose absorption after a meal, which is helpful because if your body absorbs glucose too fast, it causes the pancreas to produce extra insulin.

Cabbage: A great source of vitamin C, cabbage also may detoxify your body and help your brain function at its highest level.

Carrots: Known for their assistance in maintaining eye health, carrots also contain vitamin A, which can help liver function.

Cashews: These nuts are known to work wonders on heart, bone, hair, and skin health.

Cauliflower: Glucosinolate, a compound that can fight off certain types of cancer, especially uterine and colorectal, is found in cauliflower.

Chia seeds: Containing magnesium, iron, calcium, and potassium, these little miracle seeds also have essential fatty acids, which the body doesn't make on its own, but needs.

Chickpeas/chickpea flour: Linked to a reduced risk of heart disease, chickpeas are high in calcium, protein, and fiber. Made from ground chickpeas, the flour is packed with protein, dietary fiber, and iron.

Chives: Chives are high in vitamins A and C and packed with antioxidants.

Cilantro: Cilantro contains high levels of carotenoids, which are a great source of vitamin A.

Cinnamon: This spice can lower blood sugar and bad cholesterol levels as well as benefit people with type 2 diabetes by lowering their triglycerides.

Cocoa: Cocoa is high in antioxidants and flavonoids, which can help lower blood pressure and improve circulation.

Coconut oil: This heart-healthy oil has a lot of benefits, such as improving thyroid function, reducing cholesterol levels, and boosting your immune system.

Cranberries: Cranberries help reduce the risk of heart disease and improve oral health. They can even help prevent ulcers as well as certain kinds of cancers.

Cumin: This spice contains antioxidants that have anti-inflammatory benefits.

Dill: Loaded with amino acids and minerals, dill may help calm the body to rest easier at night.

Edamame: With its ability to lower cholesterol due to its high content of phytosterols, edamame also supplies a significant amount of protein along with fiber and folate.

Eggs: A great source of omega-3 fatty acids, which your heart will appreciate, eggs also provide large amounts of protein at a low-calorie cost.

Flaxseeds: Aside from being high in fiber, flaxseeds may fight off certain types of cancers, such as those of the breast and prostate.

Garlic: A natural antidote to high blood pressure, garlic can be helpful in warding off heart disease.

Ginger: An ancient, natural remedy, ginger has anti-inflammatory compounds and can help calm an upset stomach.

Goji berries: An ancient Chinese remedy, goji berries promote better circulation and boost the immune system. They are loaded with vitamin C and also have anti-aging claims, although not proven.

Greek yogurt: Greek yogurt naturally contains probiotics, which can improve digestion and boost your immune system.

Green tea: For centuries, people have been using green tea to treat everything from cancer to heart disease because of its high antioxidant content.

Hazelnuts: In addition to being high in fiber, folate, and vitamin E, hazelnuts have essential fatty acids that help prevent coronary artery diseases.

Honey: Raw local honey is best because it has antioxidants and has been linked to reducing allergy symptoms.

Jerusalem artichokes: Also known as sunchokes, these are loaded with fiber and thiamine, which help with muscle functioning.

Jicama: A great source of vitamin C, jicama also contains inulin, a particular fiber that promotes the growth of good bacteria in the gut.

Kale: Kale is a great source of so much: antioxidants, fiber, calcium, and iron, to name a few!

Leeks: Leeks may help protect the stomach and digestive system from gastric cancers.

Lemons and limes: These citrus fruits can help with indigestion and constipation.

Lentils: Because of their high protein and iron levels, along with other nutrients, lentils make a great choice for vegetarians—and meat eaters, too!

Mangoes: This tropical fruit is known to promote digestion and improve the immune system.

Mint: A great source of vitamins C and A, peppermint can also help with digestion.

Miso: Amino acids, organic compounds that your body needs but doesn't make on its own, can be found in miso. Miso has also been linked to reducing the risk of certain cancers.

Mushrooms: Mushrooms contain high levels of potassium as well as antioxidants, which can promote good organ function and may help ward off Parkinson's and Alzheimer's diseases.

Mustard greens: These are a great source of vitamin K, which helps keep blood, bones, and tissues healthy.

Oats/oat flour: The health claims of oats are vast, and they are believed to help reduce bad cholesterol and improve digestion. Oats are also high in fiber and antioxidants.

Olives/olive oil: This fruit is composed of healthy fats for a healthy heart.

Onions: Onions may ward off germs because of their antibiotic properties. They've been linked to lowering both blood pressure and cholesterol levels.

Oranges: In addition to supplying vitamin C, oranges may help you avoid diabetes and kidney stones as well as help decrease arthritis pain.

Oregano: This herb has one of the highest levels of antioxidants.

Oysters: High in iron, zinc, and selenium, oysters help keep the immune system in good shape.

Parsley: Containing many vitamins and minerals, this herb is also linked to building up the body's resistance to tumors.

Peanuts/peanut butter: Technically a legume, peanuts are a great source of protein, good fats, potassium, and fiber.

Pecans: These nuts may lower cholesterol levels and are one of the best sources of B complex vitamins; they provide the essential minerals calcium, zinc, potassium, and manganese.

Peppers: High in vitamin C, red peppers also contain antioxidants and can help maintain good cholesterol levels.

Pineapples: Eyes and gums can benefit from the vitamins and minerals in pineapples.

Pomegranates: This fruit may help fight off breast, prostate, and lung cancers and is also known to prevent cholesterol buildup in the arteries.

Pumpkin/pumpkin seeds: High in beta-carotene, pumpkin can help give your immune system a boost as well as help maintain the health of your eyes. The seeds are high in magnesium, protein, and omega-3 fatty acids. Some studies show a link between pumpkin seeds and strengthened muscles.

Quinoa: A superfood through and through, quinoa is the only grain that provides all nine essential amino acids that our bodies aren't able to naturally produce, making it a "complete protein." It's a great vegetarian protein option.

Red wine: With its strong antioxidants, red wine has been tied to helping fight off various forms of cancer as well as preventing blood clots.

Rosemary: This herb has been linked to a healthier heart and can help reduce inflammation.

Sage: This herb may lower cholesterol levels as well as help prevent heart disease.

Salmon: Naturally full of omega-3 fatty acids, salmon may reduce heart disease risk, lower cholesterol levels, and even help with memory loss.

Sardines: Sardines are high in vitamin D, which helps the body absorb other important minerals.

Sesame seeds/sesame oil: High levels of calcium and zinc can be found in these seeds and their oil.

Spelt flour: This ancient grain, as well as sprouted spelt flour, can be more easily digested than other types of wheat and is a good source of both iron and protein.

Spinach: Spinach provides high levels of vitamin K and calcium, which means that bones and eyes benefit the most from this leafy green.

Sprouts and microgreens: Sprouts and the sprouted seeds of vegetables (microgreens) are thought to be more nutritionally dense than their ordinary brethren.

Strawberries: Loaded with vitamin C, which can help keep your eyes in good shape, this berry also has antioxidants that can help promote a healthy immune system.

Sweet potatoes: This root is a great source of many vitamins and minerals, including iron, magnesium, and vitamins D, C, and B_6.

Swiss chard: A good source of vitamin E and folate, Swiss chard may help protect the brain from disease.

Tarragon: This herb aids digestion, and the ancient Greeks chewed on it for toothache relief.

Tofu: A great source of protein, fiber, vitamins, and minerals, tofu can also lessen the risk of developing high blood pressure and diabetes.

Tomatoes: High in lycopene, tomatoes have been known to assist almost every part of the body, including the heart, skin, eyes, and bones.

Turkey: Because it is high in protein and low in calories, turkey is a great choice for meat eaters.

Turmeric: Linked to heart health and cancer prevention, turmeric may also promote good brain function.

Walnuts: These nuts contain alpha-linolenic acid, a type of omega-3 fatty acid that's been linked to improved memory and coordination.

Watercress: High on the superfood charts, watercress is very low in calories and nutritionally dense with vitamin K, beta-carotene, and phytochemicals, which may fight off cancer.

Whole wheat flour: This flour, as well as sprouted whole wheat flour, is a great source of calcium, iron, fiber, and selenium, which helps promote immune system function.

Za'atar: This herb mix traditionally contains sumac and thyme, both of which can help lower the risk of contracting a foodborne illness.

Zucchini: Zucchini can help regulate cholesterol levels and is high in vitamin C, which makes for a strong immune system.

Part One

Foundation: Breads and Condiments

When it comes to making a sandwich, the bread choice is one of the most important aspects. It's the foundation of it all, and to make that perfect sandwich, it requires thought and attention. The bread recipes in this book range from simple (such as the Buttermilk Whole Wheat Bread on page 25), to more complex (such as the Parmesan Kale Bread on page 21). Other bread recipes use alternative flours and incorporate various vegetables, cheeses, seeds, and nuts, resulting in a more interesting and healthy sandwich.

Your recipe options really expand when you try different homemade condiments, and there are several recipes here for easy, tasty sauces, jams, butters, and spreads to accompany every sandwich.

Grocery store condiments can be loaded with additional sugars, preservatives, and other ingredients that your body just doesn't need. Plus, they can really add up in price. Making condiments at home is very simple, and the best part is that you know all that goes into making them.

I am all about the condiments. My sandwich just feels naked without them. Making condiments typically doesn't take a lot of time or energy. Unless otherwise noted, condiments also have a long shelf life and if properly stored in an airtight container in the refrigerator, they can last for two or even three weeks. For that reason, the quantities that these recipes yield are much more than you'll need for one recipe. You can use the rest for recipes you make later or for dips.

Chapter 1

Breads, Rolls, and Biscuits

PARMESAN KALE BREAD

YIELD: 1 loaf, 8 to 10 slices

I was not one of those people who loved kale—until I found new ways to introduce my taste buds to this flavorful, versatile green. Now I can't seem to get enough of it. If you're like me and need some convincing, give this recipe a shot; it may change your mind about kale. If you've already fallen under this mighty green's spell, then you'll love this bread.

2 tablespoons (30 ml) extra-virgin olive oil

2 cups (140 g) chopped kale

1 cup (235 ml) warm water

2½ teaspoons (10 g) yeast

2 teaspoons honey

Pinch of freshly grated nutmeg

1 cup (100 g) grated Parmesan cheese, divided

1½ cups (180 g) whole wheat flour

1¼ cups (210 g) all-purpose flour

1 teaspoon kosher salt

1 egg

Zest of 1 lemon

2 tablespoons (5 g) chopped fresh basil

In a small skillet over medium heat, heat the oil and add the kale. Heat the kale until it has wilted down but still is vibrantly green, 3 to 4 minutes. In a small bowl, combine the water, yeast, and honey. Stir to combine and let sit until the yeast gets foamy.

Using a stand mixer with the dough hook attachment, combine the nutmeg, ⅔ cup (65 g) of the cheese, both flours, and salt. If you don't have a stand mixer, combine these ingredients by hand in a large bowl. Add the egg and lemon zest and mix on low speed. Slowly add the yeast mixture, along with the cooked kale and basil. Knead for about 5 minutes on medium speed, or until the dough releases from the sides of the bowl and forms a ball in the center. If making dough by hand, knead the dough on a floured surface for about 10 minutes, or until the dough becomes smooth and elastic but is still a little sticky. If the dough still sticks to the sides of the bowl or to your hands and looks a little wet, add another ¼ cup (30 g) flour. Put the dough in a large, greased bowl, cover with plastic wrap, and let rest in a warm place until it doubles in size, about 1 hour.

Preheat the oven to 350°F (180°C, or gas mark 4). Once the dough has doubled in size, punch it down with your hands and lay it in a bread loaf pan. Pour the remaining ⅓ cup (35 g) cheese on top of the dough. Bake for about 45 minutes to 1 hour, or until the internal temperature of the dough is 200°F (93°C). Let cool for a couple of minutes before cutting into it. Wrap any remaining bread tightly with plastic wrap.

FEATURED SUPERFOODS:
Basil, eggs, honey, kale, lemons, olive oil, whole wheat flour

CAYENNE MAPLE SWEET POTATO BISCUITS

YIELD: 6 to 8 medium-size biscuits

Whenever I make biscuits, I wear an apron. Not because I think that I'll make a mess (even though I usually do), but because I think to make a perfect biscuit, you should be in an apron. As the dough gets kneaded, it just completes the picture—downright homey. These biscuits are enhanced with sweet potatoes and oats to give them a nutritional boost and a light, natural sweetness. That said, don't let the sweet potatoes and maple syrup throw you; these aren't super sweet biscuits. They pair beautifully with savory ingredients or are good just on their own. If you find that you want them sweeter, double the amount of maple syrup.

1¾ cups (195 g) shredded sweet potato (about 1 medium-size sweet potato)

2 teaspoons baking powder

1 teaspoon baking soda

1½ cups (120 g) old-fashioned rolled oats

1½ cups (180 g) whole wheat flour

1 teaspoon kosher salt

6 tablespoons (84 g) unsalted butter, chilled

3 tablespoons (45 ml) maple syrup

⅓ cup (80 ml) buttermilk

Pinch of cayenne pepper

Preheat the oven to 425°F (220°C, or gas mark 7). Line a baking sheet with parchment paper.

In a large bowl, combine the sweet potatoes, baking powder, baking soda, oats, and flour with your hands and add the salt. Cut the butter into small, 1-inch (2.5 cm) pieces and, using your hands, work the butter into the sweet potato and flour mixture until the butter is roughly the size of small peas.

In a separate small bowl, combine the maple syrup, buttermilk, and cayenne pepper. Pour the wet ingredients over the dry ingredients and incorporate with your hands just until the dough comes together, being careful not to overwork the dough.

Flatten the dough on a lightly floured service and cut out biscuits with a biscuit cutter or coffee cup. Lay the dough on the prepared baking sheet and bake until golden brown and firm to the touch, 10 to 12 minutes.

FEATURED SUPERFOODS:
Oats, sweet potatoes, whole wheat flour

CORNMEAL TEXAS TOAST

YIELD: 1 loaf, 8 to 10 slices

Part cornbread, part whole wheat bread, this is meant to be cut into thick slabs and toasted to create the perfect crispy vehicle for all of your sandwich needs. I find that this bread pairs exceptionally well with Mexican or Latin American sandwiches because the corn really enhances those flavors, but it's also a natural fit for sandwiches with softer ingredients that would benefit from a pop of texture.

1 cup (235 ml) milk

¼ cup (60 ml) water

1 teaspoon honey

2¼ teaspoons (9 g) yeast

⅛ teaspoon baking soda

1 teaspoon kosher salt

1 cup (120 g) all-purpose flour

1 cup (120 g) whole wheat flour

1 cup (140 g) cornmeal

1 egg

Grease a bread pan with cooking spray or olive oil. In a small bowl, combine the milk and water and heat in the microwave until the mixture is warm (or do this on the stove in a pan). Sprinkle the honey and yeast into the water-milk mixture and stir to combine. Set the mixture aside for about 10 minutes, until the yeast starts to get a little frothy.

Meanwhile, in a large bowl, combine the baking soda, salt, flours, and cornmeal. Stir to combine. Add the warm milk-yeast mixture to the flour-cornmeal mixture and stir just until combined into a thick batter. (Note: The batter will be pretty wet.) Pour the batter into the prepared bread pan, cover the pan lightly with plastic wrap, and set aside until the bread has doubled in size, about 1 hour.

Preheat the oven to 350°F (180°C, or gas mark 4). Combine the egg with a splash of water and brush on top of the bread. Bake the bread for about 30 to 40 minutes, or until it is cooked through, browned on top, and firm to the touch. Set aside to cool slightly before cutting into thick slices.

FEATURED SUPERFOODS:

Eggs, honey, whole wheat flour

BUTTERMILK WHOLE WHEAT BREAD

YIELD: 1 loaf, about 12 slices

Plain and simple, this is a great all-purpose whole wheat bread that every home cook needs. The whole wheat makes it hearty and slightly nutty, and the buttermilk gives it a pleasant tanginess. This recipe is also a great starting place for you to add your own personal touch by trying additional ingredients. Mix a cup of nuts, dried fruit, seeds, or even a grated firm cheese such as Cheddar or Parmesan into the dough at the end of the kneading process and just before you set it out to rise. There's an endless combination of flavors that you can create, so have fun with it!

2¼ teaspoons (9 g) yeast

1 teaspoon honey

¼ cup (60 ml) warm water

2 cups (240 g) whole wheat flour

1 cup (235 ml) buttermilk, plus more for brushing

1 teaspoon kosher salt

In a small bowl, combine the yeast, honey, and warm water. Set aside until the yeast starts to get foamy, 5 to 10 minutes. Using a stand mixer fitted with the dough hook attachment, combine the whole wheat flour, buttermilk, and salt. Add the yeast mixture and knead on medium-low speed until the dough comes together and pulls away from the sides of the bowl. The dough will be a bit tacky at this point, but if it is extra sticky and not pulling away from the sides of the bowl, add another ¼ cup (30 g) whole wheat flour and blend until it comes together. Spray a big bowl with cooking spray, place the dough in the center of the bowl, and drape a towel on top. Place in a warm, dry spot for about 1 hour, or until the dough doubles in size.

Preheat the oven to 375°F (190°C, or gas mark 5) and grease a bread loaf pan with cooking spray. Punch the dough down and shape in the loaf pan. Drape a towel over the loaf pan and let the dough rise in a warm, dry spot until it doubles in size, 20 to 30 minutes. Brush the top of the dough with buttermilk and bake for 45 minutes to an hour, taking it out of the oven halfway through the cooking time and brushing the top of the bread again with buttermilk. The bread is done when it is a deep golden brown and registers an internal temperature of 200°F (93°C).

FEATURED SUPERFOODS:
Honey, whole wheat flour

HONEY MISO WHOLE WHEAT SESAME BUNS

YIELD: 6 to 8 buns

Miso, fermented soybean paste, is what gives these buns a unique flavor. Five-spice powder, a Chinese blend of five to seven spices (traditionally star anise, clove, cinnamon, ginger, nutmeg, fennel, and Szechuan peppercorns), is also in the mix. This powder is thought to have been the result of someone trying to produce a "wonder blend" that included all five flavors—sour, bitter, sweet, salty, and savory. Though these buns are made from common Asian ingredients, don't feel like they are only fit for Asian meals. They're more versatile than you might think. You can also omit the five-spice powder for a more all-purpose bun if you wish. If you don't have black and white sesame seeds, use whatever you have on hand and, of course, you could omit them altogether, but they lend a nice nuttiness to the finished bread and look beautiful, adding a lot of character to any sandwich.

1 cup (235 ml) warm water

2¼ teaspoons (9 g) yeast

1½ teaspoons honey

1 tablespoon (15 ml) sesame oil

1 teaspoon five-spice powder

2½ teaspoons white miso paste

½ teaspoon kosher salt

1½ teaspoons black sesame seeds, plus more for the top

1½ teaspoons white sesame seeds, plus more for the top

2¼ cups (270 g) whole wheat flour

1 egg

Line a baking sheet with parchment paper. Combine the warm water, yeast, and honey in a small bowl. Stir to combine and set aside until the yeast starts to foam, 5 to 10 minutes. Using a stand mixer fitted with a dough hook, combine the oil, five-spice powder, miso, salt, and both sesame seeds. Add the water-yeast mixture to the bowl, and then add the flour. Knead for about 5 minutes, until the dough comes together and is elastic.

If you don't have access to a stand mixer, you can make this by hand by combining the sesame oil, five-spice powder, miso, salt, and both sesame seeds in a large bowl. Add the water-yeast mixture and then the flour and combine with your hands or a spoon. Once the dough comes together, transfer it to a clean work surface and knead the dough for about 10 minutes, or until it's smooth and elastic.

Spray a large bowl with cooking spray. Place the dough in the bowl and cover with plastic wrap. Let the bowl sit in a warm place until the dough rises and doubles in size, about 30 minutes to 1 hour. Once the dough has doubled in size, punch it down with your hand. Turn out the dough onto a clean working surface and divide into 8 equal pieces. Roll each piece into a tight bun with your hands and using your palm, flatten the bun a bit. Repeat for each bun. Place them on the prepared baking sheet and cover with plastic wrap.

Preheat the oven to 400°F (200°C, or gas mark 6) and allow the dough to rise again and double in size, about another 30 minutes.

Remove the plastic wrap from the buns. In a small bowl, combine the egg and a splash of water. Use a pastry brush to evenly coat the top of each bun with the egg wash, being careful not to get too much on the paper or at the bottom where the dough meets the paper, which can cause it to stick and burn. Sprinkle each bun with the sesame seeds and bake for about 15 minutes, or until the internal temperature of the rolls reaches 200°F (93°C).

FEATURED SUPERFOODS:

Eggs, honey, miso, sesame oil/seeds, whole wheat flour

BUCKWHEAT CARAWAY BEET BREAD

YIELD: 1 loaf, 8 to 10 slices

My maiden name in Polish translates to "beet soup" and because of that, beets always hold a special place with me. Their shockingly bright color and natural sweetness make them really fun to use when baking. This bread marries caraway seeds with buckwheat flour, which has so much depth of flavor. The shredded beets supply an irresistible, earthy sweetness. Think of this as rye bread enhanced with a pretty, magenta hue, thanks to the beets. Also, if you're not a huge fan of the taste of beets, this is a great way to get them into your diet.

½ cup (120 ml) warm water

2¼ teaspoons (9 g) yeast

1 tablespoon (20 g) honey

2 cups (450 g) shredded beets (about 1 medium-size beet, outer skin removed)

1 cup (120 g) buckwheat flour

2¼ cups (270 g) whole wheat flour

2 eggs

2 teaspoons caraway seeds

1 teaspoon kosher salt

1 teaspoon deli rye flavoring (optional)*

¼ cup (35 g) dried currants

* See Resources, page 171.

In a small bowl, combine the water, yeast, and honey. Stir with a spoon and set aside, allowing the yeast to foam up, 5 to 10 minutes. In a stand mixer fitted with the bread hook attachment, combine the beets and flours on low speed. If you don't have a stand mixer, you can make this by hand by combining the beets and flours in a large bowl using your hands or a big spoon. (If you use your hands, wear gloves to avoid your hands being dyed hot pink from the beets!) Add the yeast mixture, eggs, caraway seeds, salt, deli rye flavoring (if using), and currants. Combine either in the stand mixer or by hand until the dough comes together in one cohesive mass (about 3 to 5 minutes for the mixer, 10 to 12 minutes by hand). At this point, the dough will be tacky but it shouldn't be overly sticky. If it is, add another ¼ cup (30 g) whole wheat flour. Spray a large bowl with cooking spray, place the dough in the center, and cover with a cloth. Put in a warm place and allow to rise until it doubles in size, about 1 hour.

Preheat the oven to 375°F (190°C, or gas mark 5). Punch the dough down with your hands. Spray a loaf pan with cooking spray and lay the dough in it. Cover with a cloth and let sit in a warm area until it doubles in size again, about 30 minutes. Bake the bread until it browns on the outside and the internal temperature registers 200°F (93°C), about 35 to 40 minutes. Allow to cool a bit before slicing. Wrap any leftover bread tightly in plastic and store in the refrigerator, where it will keep for up to 1 week.

FEATURED SUPERFOODS:
Beets, buckwheat, eggs, honey, whole wheat flour

SPELT AND FLAXSEED CHALLAH

YIELD: 1 large loaf (about 20 slices) or 2 small loaves (about 10 slices per loaf)

Challah, the classic braided Jewish bread that is known for its sweet eggy flavor, gets a makeover in this recipe. Spelt flour, which lends a subtle nuttiness and is high in fiber and iron, is a great addition not only nutritionally speaking but also because it brings a little complexity to the overall flavor. Flaxseeds add texture and a second blast of nutrition.

2¼ teaspoons (9 g) yeast

½ cup (120 ml) warm water

½ cup (160 g) honey

2½ cups (300 g) spelt flour

1½ cups (180 g) all-purpose flour

5 eggs

1 teaspoon kosher salt

3 tablespoons (22 g) flaxseeds, plus more for the top

1 egg yolk

In a small bowl, combine the yeast, warm water, and honey with a whisk. Let it sit until it gets foamy, about 10 minutes.

In a separate bowl, combine the flours. Using a stand mixer fitted with the dough hook, combine the eggs, salt, and flaxseeds. Pour in the yeast mixture, and then gradually add the flour. The end result will be sticky, but if the dough is too sticky, add another ½ cup (60 g) all-purpose flour. If making by hand, combine the flours in a separate bowl and then gradually add them to a large bowl that contains the eggs, salt, flaxseed, and yeast mixture. Combine with your hands and then turn out the dough onto a floured work surface and knead until it is very elastic, 8 to 10 minutes. Spray a big bowl with cooking spray and add the dough to the bowl. Cover with plastic wrap and leave to rise in a warm place until doubled in size (about 45 minutes to 1 hour).

Preheat the oven to 375°F (190°C, or gas mark 5). Punch down the dough with your fist. Place the dough on a floured work surface and divide into 3 equal pieces. Roll each piece into a long rope. Pinch the three ends of the ropes together, ball up tightly, and spread out the three strands. Braid the strands and then secure the ends by balling up the dough tightly. Spray a piece of plastic wrap with nonstick cooking spray, cover the dough with it, and allow it to rise again until doubled in size, about 30 minutes.

In a small bowl, combine the egg yolk with a splash of water and use a pastry brush to evenly coat the outside of the bread with the egg wash. Sprinkle the top with the flaxseeds and bake until the outside is golden brown and the center of the bread registers 200°F (93°C), about 1 hour.

FEATURED SUPERFOODS:
Eggs, flaxseeds, honey, spelt flour

MIDDLE EASTERN–SPICED OAT AND FLAXSEED BUNS

YIELD: 6 buns

We are fortunate enough to have near us several Middle Eastern markets with rows of colorful spices, bags of grains and pita bread, and refrigerators full of feta cheese. These buns are inspired by my visits to the markets and are dusted with a blend of Middle Eastern spices. The oat flour and flaxseed meal, which you can easily make yourself by blending them until a flour forms, give these buns a natural sweetness and heartiness. If you can't find the spices called for, you can add your favorite spices instead, or you can leave them out entirely and still have a great foundation for a satisfying sandwich.

2 tablespoons (40 g) honey

¾ cup (180 ml) warm water

2¼ teaspoons (9 g) yeast

1 cup (120 g) oat flour

1 cup (120 g) all-purpose flour

½ cup (60 g) flaxseed meal

1 teaspoon kosher salt

1 egg

1 teaspoon sumac

½ teaspoon nigella seeds

½ teaspoon Aleppo pepper

In a small bowl, combine the honey, warm water, and yeast. Let sit for about 10 minutes, or until it gets foamy. In a stand mixer fitted with the dough hook, combine the flours, flaxseed meal, and salt, and then add in the yeast mixture. Mix on medium speed until the dough comes together, scraping the sides of the bowl as needed. Continue mixing until it is smooth and no longer sticks to the bottom of the bowl. (If you don't have a stand mixer, you can do this by hand.) Spray a large bowl with nonstick cooking spray and add the dough. Cover with plastic wrap or a damp towel and let rise in a warm area until it has doubled in size, 45 minutes to 1 hour.

Preheat the oven to 375°F (190°C, or gas mark 5). Line a baking sheet with parchment paper. Take out the dough and place it on a large cutting board. Cut it into 6 equal pieces and shape them into rolls. Cover the rolls with plastic wrap or a damp towel and allow to rise until doubled in size, 20 to 30 minutes.

Make an egg wash by mixing the egg with a splash of water in a small bowl. Place the rolls on the prepared baking sheet and brush with the egg wash. Sprinkle each roll with the sumac, nigella seeds, and Aleppo pepper. Bake the rolls until golden and cooked through and reach an internal temperature of 200°F (93°C), 20 to 25 minutes.

FEATURED SUPERFOODS:
Flaxseeds, honey, oats

SEMOLINA QUINOA FOCACCIA

YIELD: 8 to 10 pieces

Most focaccia breads are a little too oily for my liking, so I set out to create one that wasn't as greasy but didn't compromise on the spongy-soft texture that makes focaccia so good. This version is chewy and light, and the addition of uncooked quinoa gives it a crunchy texture. This bread is a perfect match for sandwiches that are stuffed with softer ingredients, such as mushrooms, tomatoes, or eggplant. Try making it with different herbs for a little variety.

2½ teaspoons yeast

1 tablespoon (20 g) honey

1 cup (235 ml) warm water

1 cup (173 g) quinoa, rinsed and drained

1 cup (120 g) semolina flour

1 cup (120 g) all-purpose flour

1 teaspoon kosher salt

¼ cup (60 ml) extra-virgin olive oil

1 teaspoon chopped fresh rosemary

Spray a 9-inch (23 cm) pie plate with nonstick cooking spray or brush lightly with oil. In a small bowl, combine the yeast, honey, and warm water. Set aside until it gets foamy, about 10 minutes.

Using a stand mixer fitted with the dough hook, combine the quinoa, both flours, and the salt. Add the yeast mixture and knead the dough for about 3 to 5 minutes, or until it all comes together. If doing by hand, add the quinoa, both flours, and salt to a large bowl. Stir in the yeast mixture and bring it together with your hands until a dough forms. On a floured work surface, knead the dough with your hands for 7 to 10 minutes, or until it's smooth and elastic. Place the dough in a bowl and cover with plastic wrap. Allow to rise in a warm, dry spot, until it has doubled in size, about 45 minutes.

Preheat the oven to 400°F (200°C, or gas mark 6). Punch the dough down with your hand and press it into the prepared pie plate. Cover the dough with plastic wrap and allow to rise a second time, until the dough has doubled in size, about 30 minutes. Using your thumb, make about 20 random indentations throughout the top of the dough. Brush the oil evenly on top of the dough and dust with the rosemary. Bake for 30 to 40 minutes, or until the top is golden brown and the internal temperature registers 200°F (93°C).

FEATURED SUPERFOODS:
Honey, olive oil, quinoa, rosemary

Chapter 2

Condiments

RED ONION CRANBERRY TARRAGON JAM

YIELD: About 2 cups (480 g)

Onion jam is so versatile. It is delicious on sandwiches, and it's also a great way to lend flavor to sauces. It's an incredible addition to a cheese plate, and a dollop on top of meat or fish adds a savory sweet-tart note, giving dishes an instant punch of flavor. Dried cranberries bring sweetness and a touch of tartness, and tarragon lends a light anise flavor. Four cups (640 g) of sliced onion will seem like a lot, but I promise you they will cook down significantly. Any leftovers freeze well. I like to divide it up into single-serving packages and freeze them—then you have the perfect amount at the ready.

4 cups (640 g) thinly sliced red onions (about 3 medium-size red onions)

2 tablespoons (30 ml) extra-virgin olive oil

½ teaspoon kosher salt, plus more to taste

1 teaspoon minced garlic

⅓ cup (80 ml) balsamic vinegar

⅓ cup (50 g) dried cranberries

1 tablespoon (11 g) Dijon mustard

1 cup (235 ml) water

1 tablespoon (4 g) chopped fresh tarragon

In a large skillet, cook the onions in the oil over medium heat. Add the salt and sweat the onions until they start to soften, about 5 minutes. Add the garlic, vinegar, cranberries, and mustard and stir to combine. Reduce the heat to low and add the water, allowing the onions to slowly caramelize. Heat the jam until the onions become very soft and sweet and the water has been completely absorbed, 45 minutes to 1 hour. Add the tarragon and season with salt. Allow to cool and then store in an airtight container in the refrigerator for up to 2 weeks. You can also freeze the remaining jam for later use.

FEATURED SUPERFOODS:
Cranberries, garlic, olive oil, onions, tarragon

BLUEBERRY-CHIPOTLE BARBECUE SAUCE

YIELD: About 2½ cups (600 g)

This is the perfect sauce to slather on top of any meat, especially if it's right off the grill. The sweetness from the blueberries plays off of the smoky heat of the chipotles and works well on grilled vegetables, too. This sauce is best to make when blueberries are abundantly in season and at their sweetest, which in Massachusetts is usually July through September. I usually find that a couple of extra dashes of raspberry vinegar, if you like your sauces vinegary like I do, right before serving really helps punch this up and bring out that bright blueberry flavor.

1 tablespoon (15 ml) extra-virgin olive oil

1 cup (160 g) diced onion

2 cups (290 g) fresh blueberries

2 chipotle peppers in adobo sauce (more if you like heat, less if you don't)

⅓ cup (106 g) molasses

1 can (6 ounces, or 168 g) tomato paste

1 teaspoon kosher salt, plus more to taste

2 cups (470 ml) water

1 tablespoon (20 g) honey

2 tablespoons (30 ml) raspberry vinegar

In a medium-size pot, heat the oil over medium heat. Sweat the onion until it softens slightly and becomes translucent, about 5 minutes. Add the blueberries, chipotle peppers, molasses, tomato paste, salt, and water. Stir to combine, and then bring the mixture to a boil over high heat. Once the mixture reaches a boil, reduce to a simmer over low heat for about 1 hour, or until the sauce thickens a bit and the onions have cooked through. Let cool slightly and transfer to a blender. Purée the mixture until combined, about 1 minute. Return the sauce to the pot and add the honey and vinegar. Season to taste with salt. The sauce will keep in the refrigerator for about 2 weeks.

FEATURED SUPERFOODS:
Blueberries, honey, olive oil, onions, peppers, tomatoes

SMOKY AND SPICY RED PEPPER PESTO

YIELD: About 1½ cups (390 g)

Many cultures have some sort of variation of this mixture of vegetables, herbs, and nuts puréed until they make a delicious condiment, dip, or sauce. The addition of nuts is a great way to sneak some extra protein into your sandwiches and make them a heartier, yet still healthy meal. This pesto is great on all meats, fish, tofu, vegetables, and eggs or just as a dip. Really, there isn't much that this isn't good on. We tend to always have some sort of version of this dip in our fridge to spread on sandwiches, dip vegetables in, or top off meats and eggs.

¼ cup (35 g) hazelnuts

¼ cup (35 g) pecans

1 red bell pepper

2 teaspoons harissa

1 tablespoon (15 ml) extra-virgin olive oil

1 tablespoon (1 g) fresh cilantro

1 tablespoon (3 g) snipped fresh chives

⅓ cup (80 ml) water

1 teaspoon lemon juice

Cayenne pepper, to taste

Kosher salt, to taste

Preheat the oven to 400°F (200°C, or gas mark 6). Spread the nuts in a single layer on a baking sheet and toast until golden brown, 10 to 15 minutes. (They can go from nice and golden brown to burned very quickly, so keep an eye on them.) Set aside to cool.

Meanwhile, roast the red pepper by placing it directly on a gas stove flame and turning the pepper with tongs until it is consistently charred on the exterior. Alternatively, you can broil the pepper, turning it regularly to char all sides. Once the pepper is charred, place it in a bowl and seal with plastic wrap. Once the pepper is cool enough to handle (about 10 minutes), peel off the charred exterior and discard it. (Don't worry if there's still a little char clinging to the pepper and do not rinse it under water; that char will add a nice element.) Using your hands, separate the stem and seeds and discard them. Add the pepper to a processor or blender. Add the toasted nuts, harissa, oil, cilantro, chives, water, and lemon juice. Blend or process until it comes together, about 30 seconds. Season with the cayenne pepper and salt to taste. Store in an airtight container in the refrigerator for about 2 weeks.

FEATURED SUPERFOODS:
Chives, cilantro, hazelnuts, lemons, olive oil, pecans, peppers

CHIPOTLE BLACK BEAN SPREAD

YIELD: About 1 ½ cups (390 g)

I created this recipe first as a dip but then later took to spreading it on sandwiches. It's very easy to pull together, and it has that perfect combination of smoky heat and warm spices. You can make it as spicy as you want by adding more chipotle. For a tamer version, omit it altogether, but you'll miss out on that smoky element that makes this spread so great. In addition to that smoky, spicy kick, it provides creaminess to sandwiches that might otherwise be a bit dry.

1½ cups (375 g) canned black beans, drained and rinsed well

2 tablespoons (30 ml) extra-virgin olive oil

Juice and zest of 1 lime

1 teaspoon ground cumin

2 chipotle peppers in adobo sauce

Kosher salt, to taste

Combine all the ingredients in a blender or food processor. Purée until smooth, adding a little water if needed to make a spreadable consistency. Season with salt to taste. This will keep in the refrigerator for up to 1 week.

FEATURED SUPERFOODS:
Beans, cumin, limes, olive oil, peppers

ROASTED STRAWBERRY BALSAMIC STEAK SAUCE

YIELD: About 2 cups (480 g)

Steak sauce is one of my favorite condiments to make and have on hand, ready to slather on grilled meats, dip roasted potatoes in, or drizzle on eggs. (It may sound weird but I assure you, it's a great pairing.) It couldn't be easier to make, and it keeps for about two weeks in the fridge. In this version, the roasted strawberries provide a jammy sweetness that practically screams out for a steak and a balmy, summer evening.

2 cups (340 g) sliced strawberries

1 tablespoon (15 ml) extra-virgin olive oil

½ cup (80 g) diced onion

1 teaspoon kosher salt

½ cup (130 g) tomato paste

⅓ cup (50 g) raisins

⅓ cup (80 ml) balsamic vinegar, plus more to taste

1 teaspoon Worcestershire sauce

½ cup (120 ml) water

Preheat the oven to 400°F (200°C, or gas mark 6). Line a baking sheet with parchment paper. Spread the sliced strawberries on the prepared baking sheet and roast in the oven until they get very soft and darken in color, 20 to 30 minutes.

While the strawberries are roasting, heat the oil in a small pot over medium heat, just for a minute or two. Add the onion and salt. Sweat the onions for 3 to 5 minutes, just until they become translucent and soften. Add the tomato paste, raisins, vinegar, and Worcestershire sauce. Stir to combine. Add the roasted strawberries and the water. At this point, the sauce should be sort of loose. If it's very pasty, add another ¼ to ½ cup (60 to 120 ml) water, until it gets to the point where it looks slightly too liquidy. Bring the mixture to a boil, lower the heat, and simmer the sauce, uncovered, for about 30 minutes, stirring every so often, until it reduces by about half and thickens. Set the mixture aside to cool, and then process in a blender to a smooth consistency. The sauce should have a slight tang to it; season to taste with salt and, if needed, another splash of balsamic vinegar. Refrigerate extra sauce in an airtight container. This will keep for about 2 weeks.

FEATURED SUPERFOODS:
Olive oil, onion, strawberries, tomato

TOMATILLO YOGURT SAUCE

YIELD: About 1½ cups (360 g)

This sauce is one of my favorites to make. Tomatillos, if you haven't had them or worked with them before, have this addicting tang that is greatly enhanced by the addition of lime and cilantro. They look like green tomatoes wrapped in a papery skin, which you have to peel away before you roast them. In this sauce, yogurt rounds everything out, giving it creaminess and cooling things down, making it a perfect match for a sandwich with some heat to it. To make this sauce vegan, just omit the yogurt. This recipe makes a fair amount, which is good, because it also doubles as a great dip for tortilla chips or fresh vegetables. If you can't find fresh tomatillos, it's sometimes easier to find canned ones in the international aisle of a grocery store.

5 or 6 medium-size tomatillos, papery husks removed

2 tablespoons (30 ml) extra-virgin olive oil

Juice and zest of 1 lime

1 small bunch cilantro

1 cup (240 g) plain Greek yogurt

Kosher salt, to taste

Preheat the oven to 425°F (220°C, or gas mark 7) and line a sheet pan with parchment paper. Wash the tomatillos and place them on the lined sheet pan. Drizzle the oil on top and bake the tomatillos until they have browned and shriveled up a bit and given off some of their liquid, 20 to 30 minutes. Remove from the oven and set aside until cool enough to handle.

In a food processor or blender, add the tomatillos and their liquid along with the rest of the ingredients, except the salt. Purée until smooth and well combined, about 30 seconds. Season to taste with salt. This will keep in the refrigerator for about 1 week.

FEATURED SUPERFOODS:
Cilantro, Greek yogurt, limes, olive oil

BASIL-AVOCADO "MAYO"

YIELD: About 2 cups (480 g)

I debated a lot about what to call this recipe because it acts like a mayo, with a rich and thick texture that adds moisture and flavor. But I've never been a fan of mayonnaise, and I use this spread for so much more than just a simple condiment; however, calling it a "mayo" just seemed to make the most sense for this book. We regularly make this as a dip for dunking tortilla chips or vegetables. It's especially good in the summertime, chilled and with a small baguette, or, of course, for sandwiches. It's much healthier than a traditional mayonnaise by relying on the healthy fat from avocados. If you make it in the summer, wrap whatever you don't finish extra tightly because it can get brown in humid weather. I find if you put it in a bowl and place plastic wrap down on top, just so it's touching the "mayo" itself, it will keep a lot longer.

2 avocados

½ cup (120 ml) water

¼ cup (10 g) fresh basil

1 tablespoon (6 g) lime zest

3 tablespoons (45 ml) lime juice

1½ teaspoons kosher salt, plus more to taste

Cut the avocados in half all around the outside until your knife reaches the pit and you can smoothly cut around and separate the avocado halves. Place the side of the avocado that has a pit in the palm of your hand. Using your knife, carefully whack the knife into the pit, shaking it free. Discard the pit and use a spoon to scoop out the flesh, or just use your fingers to peel around the outside. Slice the avocado into chunks and place in a food processor or blender. Add the water, basil, lime zest, lime juice, and salt. Blend or process until the mixture is very smooth and has a mayo-like consistency. Place in a bowl with a tight-fitting lid. Refrigerate until ready to use.

FEATURED SUPERFOODS:
Avocados, basil, limes

BEET GREENS AND PECAN PESTO

YIELD: About 1½ cups (390 g)

This is a great way to use the greens that are attached to beets, if you happen to buy them as a full bunch. Eaten raw, the beet greens can be tough and bitter, but just by blanching them quickly in some salted water, they soften and become more flavorful. You can use this pesto in a variety of ways. As a coating for potatoes, it really gives them personality; as a spread, it pairs nicely with earthy portobello mushrooms.

½ cup (75 g) pecans

½ teaspoon salt, plus more to taste

2 cups (140 g) roughly chopped beet greens

½ cup (120 ml) extra-virgin olive oil

1 teaspoon lemon juice

Preheat the oven to 400°F (200°C, or gas mark 6). Spread the pecans in a single layer on a baking sheet, and toast them until golden brown, 7 to 10 minutes. Remove from the oven and set aside to cool.

Bring a pot of salted water to a boil. In a large bowl, combine 12 ice cubes with water. Once the salted water comes to a rolling boil, add the beet greens to the pot and boil them for 2 to 3 minutes. Use a slotted spoon to remove them from the boiling water and submerge in the bowl of ice water. Let them cool for about 30 seconds before removing them and transferring directly to either a blender or food processor. Add the toasted pecans and ½ teaspoon salt and secure the lid. Drizzle in the oil and add the lemon juice, processing to a smooth consistency. Season to taste with salt.

FEATURED SUPERFOODS:
Beet greens, lemons, olive oil, pecans

ROSEMARY HARD CIDER APPLE BUTTER

YIELD: 2 cups (480 g)

Apple butter always reminds me of my grandmother. She introduced me to it when I was a kid, and one of my favorite memories with her is enjoying a breakfast of thick slices of raisin bread slathered with apple butter. I always make it whenever we find ourselves with an excess of apples on hand. This version is not traditional, like the one I had with my grandmother, but I think she'd still approve. It's made with hard cider, which gives it depth of flavor and added tartness. If you'd like, you can leave out the hard cider and just use apple cider or water.

3 cups (705 ml) your favorite flavor and variety of hard cider, divided

7 cups (1050 g) peeled and diced apples (about 5 medium-size apples)

Pinch of kosher salt

1 teaspoon minced fresh rosemary

½ teaspoon ground cinnamon

In a large pot, combine 1 cup (235 ml) of the hard cider with all of the apples. Add a pinch of salt and the rosemary and cinnamon. Bring the mixture to a boil, reduce to a simmer, and cook, stirring fairly often, until the liquid has been absorbed. Once the cider has been absorbed, add another cup (235 ml) hard cider and repeat the process of stirring and simmering until the liquid has been absorbed. Repeat this process a third time with the remaining cup of (235 ml) cider. This whole process takes about 45 minutes to 1 hour and at this point, the apples should be very soft and starting to break down. Allow them to cool for a couple of minutes, and then purée the apple mixture in a food processor or blender until smooth. Return the mixture to the pot and cook a second time over low heat, stirring regularly, until the sauce starts to darken, 30 to 45 minutes. This will keep in an airtight container in the refrigerator for up to 2 weeks.

FEATURED SUPERFOODS:

Apples, cinnamon, rosemary

Part Two
The Sandwiches

Ah, here's what we're really here for anyway, right? In the following chapters, you'll find 83 recipes for fully composed superfood sandwiches and lots of photos to accompany them. The sandwich recipes in this book are meant to feed four people (one sandwich per person). These are not meant to be beastly sandwiches that stuff you to the brim, and they may be smaller than what you are used to seeing at a deli or pizza shop. Still, they are nutritionally dense and packed with protein and fiber that will satisfy your hunger and keep you fueled for some time—no overflow needed. If you're flying solo or making a meal for two, you can either cut the recipe in half or save leftovers for another meal. On the other hand, if you're cooking for a crowd, you can double or triple (you popular guy or gal) the recipe to accommodate everyone.

Ready to get started? Here we go . . .

SUPERFOOD SPOTLIGHT:
Fruits

THREE NUT BUTTER AND ACAI BERRY JAM SANDWICH

RECOMMENDED BREAD: Buttermilk Whole Wheat; Spelt and Flaxseed Challah; wheat, oat, or whole grain bread

YIELD: 4 sandwiches, about 1½ cups (390 g) nut butter, about 2 cups (520 g) jam

No sirs and ma'ams, this is not your average PB&J, but it's just as satisfying, if not more. When I first made my own peanut butter, I quickly became hooked. It's not as creamy as supermarket brands, but it's much more flavorful and surprisingly easy to make. For extra depth of flavor and added nutrition, I like to use a couple of different nuts in my recipe, but you could always just stick with one or use a different combination. The recipe for the nut butter and the jam makes a lot and takes a little more effort, but I assure you that it's worth it. All together, this sandwich is great for an on-the-go breakfast or lunch.

NUT BUTTER

1 cup (145 g) hazelnuts

1 cup (145 g) walnuts

1 cup (145 g) peanuts

2 tablespoons (40 g) honey

1 teaspoon cinnamon

1 teaspoon kosher salt

2 tablespoons (30 ml) olive oil

JAM

12 ounces (336 g) blackberries

7 ounces (196 g) unsweetened acai berry concentrate*

2 cups (340 g) chopped strawberries

2 tablespoons (40 g) honey, or to taste

To make the nut butter: Preheat the oven to 375°F (190°C, or gas mark 5). Combine all of the nuts on a baking sheet and bake for 15 to 20 minutes, shaking them regularly to ensure even toasting. The nuts are done when they are an even, deep golden brown. Set aside to cool.

Once cool, put them into a food processor or blender. Add the honey, cinnamon, and salt. Start the blender or processor, slowly streaming in the oil. Process for about 5 minutes, stopping every minute or so to scrape down the sides of the processor. The nut butter is done when it is thoroughly combined and reaches a thick consistency.

To make the jam: Combine all of the ingredients in a medium-size pot over medium-low heat. The fruit will release its moisture, and the mixture will be very wet. Keep cooking it down until it thickens and gets very jammy, 30 to 45 minutes. Remove from the heat and let cool. The jam will continue to thicken as it cools. Taste and if you'd like it sweeter, add more honey until it reaches the desired level of sweetness. Store in an airtight container in the refrigerator for up to 1 week.

Acai concentrate is available in the freezer section of most health food stores. If you can only find sweetened, adjust the honey level or omit it entirely, depending on how sweet you'd like it.

SANDWICH

8 slices bread

¼ cup (65 g) Three Nut Butter
(page 48)

¼ cup (65 g) Acai Berry Jam
(page 48)

To make the sandwich: Lay out the bread. Slather each of 4 slices with 1 tablespoon (16 g) of the nut butter. Spread the remaining 4 slices with the jam. Join each nut butter slice of bread with each jam-covered piece of bread to make 4 sandwiches. Additionally, you can toast the sandwiches in a toaster oven once they are assembled for a warm version.

FEATURED SUPERFOODS:

Acai berries, blackberries, cinnamon, hazelnuts, honey, olive oil, peanuts, strawberries, walnuts

GRILLED PINEAPPLE AVOCADO SANDWICH

RECOMMENDED BREAD: Cornmeal Texas Toast,
Buttermilk Whole Wheat Bread, hearty grain bread

YIELD: 4 sandwiches

Grilling fruits makes them look pretty by accenting them with dramatic, dark grill lines, and it also helps their sugars concentrate for an intensely flavored end result. While you can grill inside using a grill pan, if you grill the pineapple on an outdoor grill, you'll also pick up traces of smokiness. This minimal effort sandwich is a great choice for a lazy summer day when you want to keep the heat outside.

8 (1-inch, or 2.5 cm) sliced pineapple rings

1 avocado

1 tablespoon (15 ml) lime juice

8 slices bread

½ cup (8 g) fresh cilantro leaves

½ cup (75 g) sliced almonds

Grill the pineapple using either an indoor grill or an outside one. If using an outside grill, heat the grill until very hot, about 15 minutes. Scrape the grill grates clean using a grill brush. Lay the pineapple rings on the grill and cook them with the grill closed for 5 to 7 minutes on each side, until you get nice grill marks. Set aside to cool.

If using an indoor grill, preheat a grill pan over high heat for about 5 minutes. Add the pineapple to the grill pan and sear the outside, 5 to 7 minutes on each side, until grill marks develop. Set aside to cool.

Peel, pit, and cut the avocado into thin slices. Pour the lime juice over it and coat it entirely to prevent browning.

To assemble the sandwiches, lay out the bread. Top each of 4 slices with 2 rings of grilled pineapple. Divide up the avocado slices and add on top of the pineapple. Top each with equal parts cilantro and almonds. Top each half with the remaining slices of bread.

FEATURED SUPERFOODS:
Almonds, avocados, cilantro, limes, pineapples

GINGER HOISIN–GLAZED PORK TENDERLOIN SANDWICH WITH MANGO-BLUEBERRY-JICAMA SLAW

RECOMMENDED BREAD: Cornmeal Texas Toast, sub rolls, Spelt and Flaxseed Challah

YIELD: 4 sandwiches

Hoisin sauce is very easy to find in the Asian section of most grocery stores. It gets added to the pork after it cooks so that it doesn't burn during the cooking process, but the end result is sticky-sweet pork that is complemented by the fruitiness of the salsa. The ginger stands out and pairs nicely with the slaw, where the jicama adds a satisfying crunch and the fruit sweetens up and helps tame the heat from the jalapeño.

1½ pounds (680 g) pork tenderloin

1 teaspoon kosher salt

½ teaspoon black pepper

1 tablespoon (15 ml) extra-virgin olive oil

½ cup (120 ml) hoisin sauce

1 teaspoon freshly grated ginger

1 mango, cut into matchstick-size sticks

1 cup (130 g) matchstick-size sticks jicama

1 cup (145 g) blueberries

1 teaspoon lime zest

2 teaspoons lime juice

½ teaspoon honey

¼ cup (4 g) fresh cilantro, roughly chopped

1 jalapeño, diced, or to taste

8 slices bread

Preheat the oven to 400°F (200°C, or gas mark 6). Season the pork with salt and pepper. Heat the oil in a large ovenproof skillet over medium-high heat. Add the pork to the skillet and sear the outside of the pork for 5 to 7 minutes on each side. Transfer the skillet to the oven to cook the pork through, until it reaches an internal temperature of 140° to 145°F (60° to 63°C).

Combine the hoisin sauce with the ginger in a small bowl. Brush the pork with hoisin-ginger sauce and set aside to rest, about 5 minutes.

Meanwhile, combine the mango, jicama, and blueberries in a medium-size bowl. Add the lime zest, lime juice, honey, cilantro, and jalapeño. Stir to combine.

To assemble, slice the pork thinly. Lay the pork on 4 of the bread slices, divide the hoisin-ginger sauce evenly among the sandwiches, and top with the slaw and the remaining bread.

FEATURED SUPERFOODS:
Blueberries, cilantro, ginger, honey, jicama, limes, mangoes, olive oil, peppers

APPLE CINNAMON WAFFLE SANDWICH

RECOMMENDED BREAD: Waffles

YIELD: 4 sandwiches

These sandwiches can be made with your favorite waffle recipe, or, if you're in a hurry, you can use some good frozen waffles. I prefer whole wheat here because I like the extra nutty flavor. Although this sandwich can be enjoyed all year-round, it's ideal for fall and winter months. It's great to enjoy right away while it's warm and toasty, but it's also good to stash away and enjoy on the go.

2 apples

⅓ cup plus 2 tablespoons (110 ml) apple cider, divided

2 teaspoons brown sugar

1½ teaspoons ground cinnamon, divided

4 ounces (112 g) cream cheese, at room temperature

8 whole wheat waffles, toasted

Core and thinly slice the apples and add them to a medium-size skillet. Pour in ⅓ cup (80 ml) of the apple cider and add the sugar and 1 teaspoon of the cinnamon. Cook the apples in the cider mixture over medium heat until they have softened and are very fragrant, about 10 minutes.

In a small bowl, combine the remaining 2 tablespoons (30 ml) apple cider, the remaining ½ teaspoon cinnamon, and the cream cheese. Use a rubber spatula or a spoon to combine.

To assemble, spread equal parts cream cheese onto each waffle. Divide the warm apple slices into 4 equal parts and top 4 of the waffles with the apple mixture and then with the remaining cream cheese coated waffles.

FEATURED SUPERFOODS:
Apples, cinnamon

ROASTED TOMATO, JERUSALEM ARTICHOKE, AND TOASTED HAZELNUT SANDWICH

RECOMMENDED BREAD: Parmesan Kale Bread, Spelt and Flaxseed Challah, Semolina Quinoa Focaccia, whole grain bread

YIELD: 4 sandwiches

To me, this is a perfect vegetarian sandwich. It has heartiness from the roasted Jerusalem artichokes, tang from the roasted tomatoes, crunch from the toasted hazelnuts, and an herbal accent, courtesy of the trio of mint, basil, and chives. It's the perfect balance and especially good to enjoy at the very start of spring, when Jerusalem artichokes are still in season.

2 cups (300 g) peeled and chopped Jerusalem artichoke (1-inch [2.5 cm] pieces)

1 tablespoon (15 ml) extra-virgin olive oil, divided

1 cup (150 g) cherry tomatoes

Kosher salt, to taste

½ cup (75 g) hazelnuts

Zest of 1 Meyer lemon

2 tablespoons (30 ml) Meyer lemon juice

2 tablespoons (5 g) chopped fresh basil

2 tablespoons (5 g) chopped fresh mint

1 tablespoon (3 g) chopped fresh chives

1 cup (240 g) Greek yogurt

½ teaspoon honey

8 slices bread

1 cup (70 g) spinach

Preheat the oven to 400°F (200°C, or gas mark 6). Line a baking sheet with parchment paper and pile the Jerusalem artichokes on one side. Coat with half of the oil. Make a small pile of the tomatoes on the other side of the baking sheet. Coat with the remaining oil and season both with salt. Bake until the tomatoes become golden and shrivel slightly (if done first, remove them and continue cooking the Jerusalem artichokes), 25 to 30 minutes. Cook the Jerusalem artichokes until they have no resistance when pierced with a knife, 30 to 40 minutes. Set aside to cool.

Meanwhile, in a small ovenproof skillet, toast the hazelnuts in the oven, checking them often so they don't burn, until they turn golden brown, 10 to 12 minutes. Remove from the oven and set aside to cool.

In a small bowl, combine the lemon zest and juice, basil, mint, and chives. Stir in the yogurt and the honey.

Lightly toast the bread. Spread the yogurt–herb mixture on each slice. Divide the spinach among half of the slices of bread and neatly pile on the roasted tomatoes and Jerusalem artichokes. Crush the hazelnuts with a knife and divide among the slices of bread. Top with the other slices of bread.

FEATURED SUPERFOODS:
Basil, chives, Greek yogurt, hazelnuts, honey, Jerusalem artichokes, lemons, mint, olive oil, spinach, tomatoes

MIDDLE EASTERN POMEGRANATE CHICKEN SANDWICH

RECOMMENDED BREAD: Buttermilk Whole Wheat Bread, Middle Eastern–Spiced Oat Flaxseed Buns, sub rolls, whole grain bread

YIELD: 4 sandwiches

Za'atar is a popular Middle Eastern spice blend that includes sumac, dried herbs (most often dried thyme, oregano, and/or marjoram), and usually sesame seeds. It provides a tangy, intensely herbal note to food. Depending on where you get it from and who made the blend, you'll find a variety of spice mixes. You can buy it premade in most Middle Eastern markets as well as online, or you can blend your own mix. Pomegranate molasses is becoming more readily available and is usually found in the Asian/Middle Eastern section of the grocery store. It's essentially just pomegranate juice reduced down with some sugar until it turns into a thick syrup with an addictive tang to it.

1 tablespoon (15 ml) extra-virgin olive oil

1½ pounds (680 g) boneless, skinless chicken breast

1 tablespoon (6 g) za'atar (omit the salt if your spice blend contains it already)

1 teaspoon kosher salt

1 tablespoon (20 g) pomegranate molasses

8 slices bread

¾ cup (112 g) pomegranate seeds

1 cup (120 g) sliced cucumber

1 cup (20 g) arugula

Preheat the oven to 375°F (190°C, or gas mark 5). Heat the oil in a large skillet over medium-high heat for just a minute or two. Coat the chicken with the za'atar and salt. Lay the chicken in the hot skillet, ensuring that the pieces aren't too close together. Cook them on one side without flipping for 5 to 7 minutes, or until some nice, golden brown color starts to form. Flip them over and cook another 5 to 7 minutes. If the internal temperature isn't registering 165°F (74°C) at this point, transfer the whole skillet to the oven and finish cooking the chicken, 5 to 10 minutes. Set aside the chicken once it's done and allow it to rest for 5 to 10 minutes, and then slice it thinly and drizzle with the pomegranate molasses.

To assemble the sandwiches, lay out the bread and divide the pomegranate seeds evenly over 4 slices. Top each with ¼ cup (30 g) of the cucumbers. Divide the chicken slices among the sandwiches, top with the arugula and remaining bread slices.

FEATURED SUPERFOODS:
Arugula, olive oil, pomegranates, za'atar

CARAMELIZED ONION, APPLE, AND SMOKED GOUDA GRILLED CHEESE

RECOMMENDED BREAD: Spelt and Flaxseed Challah,
Buttermilk Whole Wheat Bread, whole wheat bread

YIELD: 4 sandwiches

Most kids sneak cookies when their mothers aren't looking or dream about cakes and ice cream. But not me. I would sneak extra cheese (sorry you had to find out about it this way, Mom) and fantasize about sharp Cheddar cheese and crackers. Cheese is, and has been, one of my favorite things on the planet to eat, and I'd take a good square of cheese over most anything. For that reason, I love grilled cheese sandwiches, but I like to lighten them up a bit by adding fruits and vegetables. I also select a healthy bread and go a little light on the cheese. This sandwich marries one of my ultimate favorite combinations in the cheese world: apples and a smoky cheese. The Rosemary Hard Cider Apple Butter finishes it off with an herbal, sweet, and savory note.

1 tablespoon (15 ml) extra-virgin olive oil

3 cups (480 g) sliced onion (about 2 large onions)

1 teaspoon kosher salt

8 slices bread

½ cup (120 g) Rosemary Hard Cider Apple Butter (page 45)

8 slices smoked Gouda

In a large skillet, heat the oil over medium heat. Add the onion and salt. Once the onions start cooking, lower the heat to medium-low and, stirring often so that they don't stick to the bottom of the pan, cook the onions slowly until they get very soft and turn golden brown, about 1 hour. Set aside to cool a bit.

Lay out the bread and coat each slice with 1 tablespoon (15 g) of the apple butter. Add 2 pieces of cheese to 4 of the bread slices and divide the caramelized onions among the other 4 bread slices. Top the onions with the apple slices. Join one side of the cheese-topped bread with one side of the caramelized onion–topped bread to create 4 sandwiches. Add the sandwiches to a large, nonstick skillet and heat over medium heat, flipping after one side starts to get color. The sandwich is done when both sides are toasted and the cheese is melted.

FEATURED SUPERFOODS:
Apples, olive oil, onions

THAI "ELVIS" SANDWICH

RECOMMENDED BREAD: Waffles, Spelt and Flaxseed Challah, oat or whole wheat bread

YIELD: 4 sandwiches

This sandwich sort of happened by mistake, and a good mistake it was! I knew that I wanted to include some sort of version of an Elvis sandwich—a classic combination of salty peanut butter and sweet, sliced bananas. I had some leftover peanut sauce, so I made some waffles, slathered it on them, and put sliced bananas on top. I also added some toasted peanuts for crunch and voilà—a sweet, salty, and spicy sandwich that turned out pretty great. This makes for a quick lunch or even a hearty midday or late-night snack for when you're craving something different.

½ cup (75 g) unsalted peanuts

½ cup (130 g) peanut butter

2 teaspoons red curry paste

¼ cup (60 ml) warm water

¼ teaspoon kosher salt

Sriracha, to taste

3 bananas

8 waffles, homemade or frozen

Preheat the oven to 400°F (200°C, or gas mark 6). Lay out the peanuts in a single layer on a baking sheet. Toast the peanuts for 7 to 10 minutes, or until they have darkened in color. Remove from the oven and set aside to cool.

In a small bowl, combine the peanut butter, red curry paste, water, and salt. Stir to combine until a smooth sauce forms. Drizzle in the sriracha to your desired spice level. Stir to combine and set aside. Slice the bananas thinly.

Lay out the waffles and spread the Thai peanut butter evenly over each one. Top 4 of the waffles with the banana slices and then the toasted peanuts. Top each with the remaining 4 waffles.

FEATURED SUPERFOODS:
Bananas, peanuts/peanut butter

CHICKEN WITH STRAWBERRY, RHUBARB, AND BASIL SALSA SANDWICH

RECOMMENDED BREAD: Sub rolls, baguette, Semolina Quinoa Focaccia

YIELD: 4 sandwiches

With so many sandwiches in this book, it is hard to play favorites, but this is a top contender. The sweetness from the strawberries and the intense tang of the rhubarb against the savoriness of the chicken make this sandwich a standout. I'm also partial to basil and strawberries together. It's a simple and straightforward sandwich that doesn't take long to put together and tastes delicious. Try making this in spring/early summer, when rhubarb and strawberries are at their best. For another layer of flavor, try adding goat cheese to the mix or crumbled feta for a salty component.

2 tablespoons (30 ml) extra-virgin olive oil

1½ pounds (680 g) boneless, skinless chicken breast

½ teaspoon salt

1 cup (170 g) diced strawberries

2 tablespoons (15 g) finely diced rhubarb

½ teaspoon honey

2 tablespoons (5 g) roughly chopped basil

4 sub rolls, sliced in half

Preheat the oven to 375°F (190°C, or gas mark 5). Heat the oil in a large ovenproof skillet over medium-high heat for 1 to 2 minutes. Season the chicken with the salt, add it to the pan, and sear it for about 5 minutes on each side. Place the pan in the oven and finish cooking the chicken, just until the internal temperature registers 165°F (74°C). Remove the chicken from the skillet and place on a clean cutting board to rest for 5 to 7 minutes. Slice thinly. The chicken can also be chilled and the sandwich enjoyed cold.

Meanwhile, prepare the salsa by combining the strawberries, rhubarb, honey, and basil in a medium bowl.

To assemble the sandwiches, lay out the sub rolls and stuff each evenly with the chicken slices. Top each sandwich with equal amounts of salsa.

FEATURED SUPERFOODS:
Basil, honey, olive oil, strawberries

STEAK AND ROASTED STRAWBERRY SANDWICH

RECOMMENDED BREAD: Sub rolls, baguette, kaiser rolls

YIELD: 4 sandwiches

To me, this sandwich tastes just like summertime should. The ingredients are simple and fresh, and roasting the strawberries, deepens their flavor and adds to the meatiness of the steak. This sandwich pairs nicely with a chilled glass of rosé, and preferably a seat outside.

1½ pounds (680 g) sirloin steak or your favorite cut of beef

1 pound (454 g) strawberries, washed, hulled, and halved

1 tablespoon (15 ml) neutral cooking oil, such as grapeseed oil

1½ teaspoons kosher salt

½ cup (120 ml) Roasted Strawberry Balsamic Steak Sauce (page 40), divided

1 cup (120 g) thinly sliced English cucumber

3 tablespoons (45 ml) raspberry vinegar

4 sub rolls, sliced in half

½ cup (35 g) microgreens, sprouts, or other lettuce

Preheat the oven to 400°F (200°C, or gas mark 6) and line a baking sheet with parchment paper. Bring the steak to room temperature by removing it from the refrigerator about 20 to 30 minutes before you plan to cook it.

Spread the strawberries on the prepared baking sheet and roast until they get very soft and darken in color, 20 to 30 minutes.

In a medium-size skillet, heat the oil until very hot, but not smoking. Dry the steak with paper towels to get rid of any excess moisture. Season the steak with the salt, coating evenly on both sides. Place the steak in the hot skillet. It should make a loud sizzling noise. If it doesn't, the pan and oil are not hot enough. If this is the case, remove the steak from the skillet and wait until the oil is hot enough. Sear the steak for 5 to 7 minutes on each side, flipping only once. After flipping, brush with ¼ cup (60 ml) of the steak sauce. Depending on the thickness of the steak and the desired doneness, it may need to be cooked longer in the oven. Using an instant-read thermometer, cook the steak until the internal temperature registers 130°F (54.5°C) for medium-rare, 140°F (60°C) for medium, and 150°F (65.5°C) for well done. Take the steak off the heat and let it rest for 5 minutes before slicing to allow the juices to redistribute.

While the steak rests, toss the cucumber with the vinegar and toast the sub rolls (optional). Thinly slice the steak. Layer the rolls with the cucumbers, steak, and strawberries, drizzle with the remaining steak sauce, and top with the microgreens. Serve immediately.

FEATURED SUPERFOODS:
Microgreens, olive oil, onions, sprouts, strawberries, tomatoes

TURMERIC CHICKPEA SANDWICH WITH CARDAMOM-SPICED APPLES

RECOMMENDED BREAD: Middle Eastern–Spiced Oat Flaxseed Buns, sub rolls

YIELD: 4 sandwiches

Although the turmeric in this sandwich gives the chickpeas a bright yellow tinge and a subtle, mustardy flavor, the real stars of the show are the apples. They are quickly marinated in champagne vinegar and cardamom so that they develop a tangy, spice-laden, almost sweet pickle–like quality while still maintaining their tart flavor. This sandwich is easy to throw together and travels well, making it an ideal choice for when you're on the go.

½ cup (75 g) diced Granny Smith apple

3 tablespoons (45 ml) champagne vinegar

¼ teaspoon cardamom

1½ cups (360 g) chickpeas, drained and rinsed if canned

1 teaspoon grated fresh ginger

½ teaspoon turmeric

4 buns or rolls, sliced in half

1 cup (20 g) arugula

1 cup (120 g) sliced cucumber

In a small bowl, combine the apple with the vinegar and cardamom. Set aside. In a separate bowl, combine the chickpeas with the ginger and turmeric.

To assemble the sandwiches, lay out the buns. Top each bottom half with equal amounts of the arugula and cucumber. Next, divide up the chickpeas among the buns, and then drain the apples of any excess vinegar and lay on top of the chickpeas. Finish with the top of the bun.

FEATURED SUPERFOODS:
Apples, arugula, chickpeas, ginger, turmeric

DAD'S GARDEN SANDWICH

RECOMMENDED BREAD: Parmesan Kale Bread, sub rolls, baguette, kaiser rolls

YIELD: 4 sandwiches

When my dad was young, he wanted to be a farmer, and that desire to grow his own fruits and vegetables stuck with him through adulthood. Our summers included many varieties of tomatoes, from little cherry tomatoes to plump beefsteak tomatoes. "So sweet you'd think they were candy!" he'd exclaim. The summertime dinners of my childhood were always accompanied by a big bowl of garden fresh, crisp cucumbers and sliced tomatoes, seasoned simply with rice wine vinegar, giving them a sweet pickle-y quality. Every summer my dad proudly presents me with a giant brown paper bag of tomatoes and cucumbers, and those summery flavors inspired this sandwich. It's best when the veggies are in season. Give them some time to marinate and allow the flavors to come together. It's perfect for a hot night when turning on the oven is not appealing.

2 cups (240 g) sliced pickling or English cucumbers

8 slices tomato

¼ cup (60 ml) rice wine vinegar

8 slices bread

8 basil leaves

In a shallow bowl, combine the cucumbers and tomatoes. Pour the rice wine vinegar over them and allow to marinate for 10 to 20 minutes before removing from the bowl and shaking off any excess vinegar.

To assemble the sandwiches, lay out the bread and divide up the cucumbers among 4 slices. Top with 2 tomato slices each and then lay 2 pieces of fresh basil on top. Finish by topping each of the sandwiches with the last slice of bread.

FEATURED SUPERFOODS:
Basil, tomatoes

FRUITY BREAKFAST SANDWICH

RECOMMENDED BREAD: Spelt and Flaxseed Challah, Buttermilk Whole Wheat Bread, waffles

YIELD: 4 sandwiches

If I say "breakfast sandwich" to you, you'll probably immediately picture an egg sandwiched in an English muffin, and I can't say I blame you. The two seem to go hand in hand, leaving little room for other types in the breakfast sandwich game. I'm not hating on egg sandwiches; they have a special place in my heart (and in this book), but sometimes I crave something a little lighter, and this refreshing fruit and yogurt sandwich does just the trick. Try swapping in other seasonal fruits to keep things interesting.

1 cup (240 g) Greek yogurt or labneh*

2 tablespoons (40 g) honey

1 tablespoon (6 g) lemon zest (zest from about 1 lemon)

¼ cup (35 g) pecans, chopped

1 grapefruit

8 slices bread

1 cup (170 g) sliced strawberries

*See Resources, page 171.

Preheat the oven to 400°F (200°C, or gas mark 6). In a small bowl, combine the Greek yogurt, honey, and lemon zest. Stir to combine and set aside.

Spread the pecans on a baking sheet in a single layer. Toast in the oven for about 10 minutes, or until the nuts are an even shade of brown. Set aside to cool.

Segment the grapefruit by cutting off the top and bottom skin, just enough until you reach the flesh, about ½ inch (1.3 cm) or so. Stand the fruit upright on a cutting board. With your knife, and working in sections, slice the skin and pith off, working along the contours of the grapefruit and revealing just the flesh. Holding the grapefruit in your hand over a bowl, carefully cut in between the membranes of the grapefruit. Shake the grapefruit flesh loose with your knife and into the bowl. Continue this process for the whole grapefruit.

Lay the bread out on a work service and spread 2 tablespoons (30 g) of the yogurt over each slice of bread. Divide the grapefruit segments among 4 slices of bread. Top with the sliced strawberries and sprinkle with the toasted pecans. Top each with the remaining 4 slices of bread.

FEATURED SUPERFOODS:
Greek yogurt, honey, lemons, pecans, strawberries

Chapter 4

SUPERFOOD SPOTLIGHT:
Greens

INDIAN GRIDDLED HALLOUMI AND SPINACH SANDWICH

RECOMMENDED BREAD: Sub rolls, Honey Miso Whole Wheat Sesame Buns

YIELD: 4 sandwiches

This sandwich is a play on the popular Indian dish *saag paneer*, which combines spinach, paneer cheese, and loads of spice. Halloumi, if you've never had it before, is one of my favorite cheeses because you can sear it over moderately high heat, and, instead of melting, it retains its shape and develops a golden and crispy exterior that enhances its flavor. It can be pretty salty in the best of ways, so a little goes a long way. If you can't find halloumi cheese, you can use the classic paneer, which can also handle the heat and be cooked like halloumi. If you can't find either, queso fresco or even feta crumbled over the sandwich right before serving would work well, too.

½ pound (226 g) halloumi cheese

1 teaspoon extra-virgin olive oil

¾ cup (120 g) diced onion

Pinch of salt

½ teaspoon minced garlic

1 teaspoon garam masala

1 teaspoon grated fresh ginger

6 cups (180 g) fresh baby spinach

4 sub rolls, sliced in half

Dice the halloumi into ½-inch (1.3 cm) cubes. Heat a dry, nonstick skillet over medium heat for about 2 minutes. Add the cheese to the skillet, making sure they are in a single layer and each cube has space to brown. (You may need to work in batches.) Heat the cheese for 1 to 2 minutes, or until it starts to turn golden brown. Using tongs, flip the cheese over and repeat the process, searing the other side of each cube. Once two sides are seared, transfer the cheese to a plate to cool

Using the same skillet, heat the oil over medium heat for a minute or two. Add the onion and salt. Cook until the onion starts to soften and becomes translucent, 3 to 5 minutes. Add the garlic and cook for another minute more. Add the garam masala and ginger. Stir to combine. Add the spinach to the skillet and cook until wilted, stirring to combine, 3 to 5 minutes. Add the halloumi back to the skillet, stir to combine, and adjust the salt if necessary.

Lay out the sub rolls and evenly divide the spinach and halloumi among the rolls.

FEATURED SUPERFOODS:
Garlic, ginger, olive oil, onions, spinach

WATERCRESS, APPLE, AND PECAN SANDWICH WITH LEMON POPPY SEED VINAIGRETTE

RECOMMENDED BREAD: Parmesan Kale Bread, Semolina Quinoa Focaccia, Buttermilk Whole Wheat Bread, Spelt and Flaxseed Challah, sub rolls

YIELD: 4 sandwiches

Watercress is a great addition to this sandwich because it has a sharp, almost horseradish-like flavor that plays well with the other sweet and tart components. Also, watercress tends to top the superfood charts with its exceptionally high nutritional value. This sandwich is easy to make for a crowd. Most ingredients may already be in your cabinet, and the poppy seed–studded vinaigrette gives it a sophisticated look. There's also a great balance of textures—crunchiness from the apple and pecans and chewiness from the dried cranberries—that makes this one hard to put down.

1 tablespoon (6 g) poppy seeds

1 teaspoon lemon zest

2 teaspoons lemon juice

1 tablespoon (20 g) honey

¼ cup (60 ml) extra-virgin olive oil

2 tablespoons (30 ml) champagne vinegar

1 apple, cut into thin matchsticks

1 cup (145 g) pecans

½ cup (75 g) dried cranberries

8 slices bread

2 cups (60 g) watercress

In a medium-size bowl, combine the poppy seeds, lemon zest and juice, honey, oil, and vinegar and whisk for a couple of seconds until it comes together in a smooth vinaigrette. Add the apple, pecans, and cranberries. Set aside until ready to use.

To assemble the sandwiches, lay out the bread and divide the watercress among 4 slices. Top with the apple and pecan mixture and the remaining slices of bread.

FEATURED SUPERFOODS:
Apples, cranberries, honey, lemons, olive oil, pecans, watercress

MEXICAN STUFFED POBLANO PEPPER SANDWICH

RECOMMENDED BREAD: Cornmeal Texas Toast, sub rolls

YIELD: 4 sandwiches

This recipe is loaded with superfoods and is so satisfying. For best results, make sure the cornmeal is a thicker texture, like the one used to make polenta, rather than the powdery, flour-like cornmeal used to make muffins.

2 poblano peppers, cut in half lengthwise, seeds and stems removed

4 cups (280 g) Swiss chard, leaves and stems separated (about 1 bunch)

1 teaspoon minced garlic

1½ cups (270 g) diced tomato

¼ cup (35 g) raisins

1 teaspoon ground cumin

½ teaspoon kosher salt

7 tablespoons (63 g) cornmeal, divided

1 cup (120 g) shredded sharp Cheddar cheese, divided

¼ cup (35 g) pumpkin seeds

8 slices bread

Preheat the oven to 450°F (230°C, or gas mark 8) and line a baking sheet with parchment paper. Lay the peppers on the baking sheet. Bake for 15 to 17 minutes, until they start to char. Remove from the oven and set aside.

Meanwhile, cut the Swiss chard stems into ½-inch (1.3 cm) pieces. Roughly chop the leaves. Blanch the stems in boiling water for 2 to 3 minutes. Add the leaves. Cook for another 1 to 2 minutes. Meanwhile, prepare a large bowl of ice water and then, once 4 to 5 minutes have passed, use a slotted spoon to remove the stems and leaves and add them to the water bath. In a little less than a minute, remove from the water, shake off any water, and set aside in a large bowl.

In a skillet, heat the oil over medium heat for 1 minute. Add the garlic and heat for another minute before adding the tomatoes. Add the raisins, cumin, and salt and let simmer, stirring regularly, 5 to 7 minutes. Remove from the skillet and combine with the Swiss chard. Add ¼ cup (36 g) of the cornmeal, ½ cup (60 g) of the cheese, and the pumpkin seeds. Stir to combine.

Lower the oven to 400°F (200°C, or gas mark 6). Divide the Swiss chard mixture among the peppers. You can serve any extra stuffing alongside the peppers, add it to the sandwiches just before serving, or reserve for another use. Top the peppers with the remaining cheese and finish by dusting the peppers with the remaining cornmeal. Place in a baking dish and bake until the cheese melts and starts to brown, 15 to 20 minutes.

To assemble the sandwiches, lay out the bread and top 4 of the slices with half of a pepper. Top with the remaining slice of bread.

FEATURED SUPERFOODS:
Cumin, garlic, peppers, pumpkin seeds, Swiss chard, tomatoes

SPINACH AND ZUCCHINI CORNMEAL CAKES WITH SPICED GOAT CHEESE

RECOMMENDED BREAD: Sub rolls, burger buns, Middle Eastern–Spiced Oat Flaxseed Buns

YIELD: 4 sandwiches

While some veggie burgers can end up mushy, the cornmeal in this one helps give this patty some texture. I like to use a coarser cornmeal so you really get that crunch. I make these a lot in the late spring and early summer months when the ingredients are in season. For more protein and texture, add chopped nuts to the mix. Consider using wilted Swiss chard or mustard greens in place of the spinach.

5 cups (150 g) fresh spinach

1½ cups (180 g) shredded zucchini (about 1 medium-size zucchini)

1 teaspoon lemon zest

1 egg

⅔ cup (92 g) cornmeal

⅓ cup (13 g) chopped basil

½ teaspoon salt

Pinch of ground black pepper

¼ cup (30 g) all-purpose flour

2 tablespoons (30 ml) extra-virgin olive oil

½ cup (120 g) goat cheese, at room temperature

1 teaspoon sumac

½ teaspoon dried mint

4 sub rolls or buns, sliced in half

In a large skillet over medium-low heat, heat the spinach until it wilts but still has its vibrant green color, about 5 minutes. (You should end up with about ½ cup [90 g] once it's all wilted.) Let it cool for a couple of minutes until it's not too hot to touch.

In a large bowl, combine the zucchini, spinach, lemon zest, and egg. Add the cornmeal, basil, salt, and pepper. Add the flour and combine until it just comes together. Don't overmix or you'll end up with tough cakes! At this point, your "batter" should look like very thick, loose cookie dough. If you find your batter is a little too loose, you can add cornmeal by the ¼ cup (35 g) until it reaches the desired consistency.

Heat the oil in a large skillet over medium-high heat for a couple of minutes. Divide the batter into 4 equal portions and drop each portion by the spoonful into the hot skillet, giving them plenty of room to spread out. Cook until golden brown, 5 to 7 minutes, and then flip them over and cook the other side until it becomes golden brown as well. Transfer the cakes to a plate and season with a little dusting of salt.

While the cakes are cooking, combine the goat cheese, sumac, and mint in a small bowl. Spread evenly over each roll. Top with a zucchini cake and enjoy.

FEATURED SUPERFOODS:
Basil, eggs, lemons, mint, olive oil, spinach, zucchini

GINGER CHICKEN SANDWICH
WITH ASIAN MUSTARD GREENS SALAD

RECOMMENDED BREAD: Honey Miso Whole Wheat Sesame Buns, rolls

YIELD: 4 sandwiches

Mustard greens are sharp in flavor and have a slight mustardy taste. They wilt beautifully and still maintain texture and their bright flavor. They are common in Asian cuisine, and this sandwich combines flavors such as ginger, soy sauce, and sesame seeds that are also common in that cuisine. Crunchy toasted peanuts finish off this sandwich.

1 teaspoon freshly grated ginger

2 teaspoons soy sauce

1 teaspoon minced garlic

1½ pounds (680 g) boneless, skinless chicken breast

½ cup (75 g) unsalted peanuts

1½ teaspoons coconut oil, divided

3 cups (210 g) stemmed, roughly chopped mustard greens

Kosher salt, to taste

½ cup (75 g) mandarin orange slices

1 teaspoon rice wine vinegar

2 teaspoons sesame seeds

4 buns or rolls, sliced in half

Preheat the oven to 375°F (190°C, or gas mark 5). In a small bowl, combine the ginger, soy sauce, and garlic. Stir until it makes a paste. Rub it evenly over the chicken and let marinate for about 10 minutes at room temperature.

Meanwhile, spread the peanuts on a baking sheet in a single layer and toast until darker in color and very fragrant, 10 to 12 minutes. Set aside to cool, and then crush them with a meat mallet or heavy skillet.

Heat 1 teaspoon of the oil in a large ovenproof skillet over medium-high heat for 1 to 2 minutes, and then add the chicken. Cook for 5 to 7 minutes, flipping once you see golden brown color. Sear the other side for 5 to 7 minutes, and then place the skillet in the oven to cook through, 5 to 7 minutes, or until the internal temperature registers 165°F (74°C). Set aside to rest for 5 minutes before slicing.

Meanwhile, heat the remaining ½ teaspoon oil in a large skillet. Add the mustard greens and season to taste with salt. Wilt the greens over medium heat, just until they start to go limp but still have their bright green color. Remove from the heat and transfer to a bowl. Add the orange slices, rice wine vinegar, and sesame seeds. Stir to combine.

To assemble, lay out the buns and divide the chicken among them. Divide the mustard green salad into 4 portions and lay on top of the chicken.

FEATURED SUPERFOODS:
Coconut oil, garlic, ginger, mustard greens, oranges, peanuts, sesame seeds

LEEK SPANAKOPITA CHICKEN SANDWICH

RECOMMENDED BREAD: Parmesan Kale Bread, Buttermilk Whole Wheat Bread,
Spelt and Flaxseed Challah, other whole grain bread

YIELD: 4 sandwiches

Growing up, I always thought that it didn't get much fancier than spanakopita, the classic Greek dish made from spinach, feta cheese, onions, and herbs, and when it was folded up into neat little phyllo triangles, I couldn't get enough. They were the height of sophistication for a little kid like me. This sandwich is a play on that, but leeks are added to the mix, giving it a sweet and delicate onion flavor. When making this, buy the best-quality feta you can get your hands on. Good feta has a more complex flavor, and its saltiness has a personality all its own.

1 tablespoon plus ½ teaspoon (17.5 ml) extra-virgin olive oil

1½ pounds (680 g) boneless, skinless chicken breast

1 teaspoon kosher salt

Ground black pepper, to taste

1 cup (105 g) halved leeks, white part only

6 cups (180 g) baby spinach

1 cup (150 g) crumbled feta cheese

½ teaspoon chopped fresh oregano

1 teaspoon chopped fresh dill

1 teaspoon lemon zest

1 teaspoon fresh lemon juice

8 slices bread

Preheat the oven to 375°F (190°C, or gas mark 5). Heat 1 tablespoon (15 ml) of the olive oil in an ovenproof skillet over medium heat. Season the chicken with the salt and pepper. Add the chicken to the skillet, searing the outside for 5 to 7 minutes, or until it develops a golden exterior. Flip the chicken over and sear the other side for another 5 to 7 minutes, or until golden brown. Transfer the skillet to the oven and bake until the internal temperature of the chicken registers 165°F (74°C), 7 to 10 minutes, depending on the size of the chicken. Remove from the oven and set aside.

In a nonstick skillet over medium heat, heat the remaining ½ teaspoon (2.5 ml) olive oil. Add the leeks and a generous pinch of salt. Cook until they soften and become translucent, about 5 minutes, before adding the spinach. (You may need to work in batches.) Wilt the spinach, just until it softens but still has its vibrant green color. Turn off the heat and add the cheese, oregano, dill, lemon zest, and lemon juice. Set aside.

Slice the chicken thinly and divide among 4 slices of bread. Top each with the leek-spinach mixture and the final slice of bread.

FEATURED SUPERFOODS:
Dill, leeks, lemons, olive oil, oregano, spinach

PORK TENDERLOIN SANDWICH WITH SHREDDED BRUSSELS SPROUT SLAW

RECOMMENDED BREAD: Sub rolls, kaiser rolls, Semolina Quinoa Focaccia, Parmesan Kale Bread

YIELD: 4 sandwiches

If you aren't a big fan of Brussels sprouts, this sandwich might make you a believer. The mustard and balsamic vinegar brighten any bitterness from the sprouts, and dried currants give it a touch of sweetness. I find that the sharper (meaning more aged) provolone works the best because the flavor stands out, but regular sliced provolone works great here, too.

½ pound (226 g) Brussels sprouts

1 tablespoon (15 ml) extra-virgin olive oil

¼ cup (35 g) currants

2 teaspoons balsamic vinegar

2 tablespoons plus 1 teaspoon (26 g) Dijon mustard, divided

Salt

1½ pounds (680 g) pork tenderloin

4 slices provolone cheese

4 sub rolls, sliced in half

Preheat the oven to 425°F (220°C, or gas mark 7). Prepare the Brussels sprouts by washing them, trimming their stems, and then shredding them into thin strips with a knife. Heat the oil in a medium-size skillet over medium-high heat and add the Brussels sprouts, currants, vinegar, and 1 teaspoon (4 g) of the mustard. Stir to combine and cook, stirring regularly, until the sprouts start to brown, 10 to 15 minutes. Season to taste with salt.

While the sprouts are cooking, rub the pork with the remaining 2 tablespoons (22 g) mustard and season generously with salt. Lay the pork in a pan and cook until the exterior is browned and the center registers an internal temperature of 140° to 145°F (60° to 63°C). Transfer to a clean cutting board to rest for 5 to 7 minutes.

To assemble the sandwich, divide the cheese evenly among the sub rolls and melt in the toaster or oven. Slice the pork thinly and divide equally among the sandwiches. Top with equal amounts of the slaw.

FEATURED SUPERFOODS:
Brussels sprouts, olive oil

MOROCCAN KALE RATATOUILLE SANDWICH

RECOMMENDED BREAD: Spelt and Flaxseed Challah, Parmesan Kale Bread,
Honey Miso Whole Wheat Sesame Buns

YIELD: 4 sandwiches

There are a couple of tricks to good ratatouille. First, you need a fair amount of garlic and olive oil. Second, cook it only until all of the vegetables are cooked through. If you cook it any longer, it starts to turn to mush. Ratatouille is a classic French dish, but I've given it an African makeover and added kale, which goes along beautifully with the other vegetables.

3 tablespoons (45 ml) extra-virgin olive oil, divided

1½ cups (240 g) diced onion

Kosher salt, to taste

1 tablespoon (10 g) minced garlic

4 cups (280 g) diced eggplant (1-inch [2.5 cm] cubes, about 1 small eggplant)

2 cups (240 g) diced zucchini (½-inch [1.3 cm] cubes, about 1 medium zucchini)

1½ cups (240 g) diced tomato (about 1 large tomato)

½ teaspoon ground cinnamon

1 teaspoon ground cumin

¼ teaspoon ground clove

1 teaspoon smoked paprika

2 cups (140 g) roughly chopped kale

8 slices bread

In a medium-size pot over medium heat, heat 1 tablespoon (15 ml) of the oil for a minute or two and then add the onion. Add about ¼ teaspoon of the salt to help the onion sweat. Cook the onion for about 5 minutes, until it starts to become translucent. Add the garlic and cook another 2 to 3 minutes. Add the eggplant next, and cook, stirring fairly regularly so that the eggplant doesn't stick to the bottom. If it does, you can just add a little more oil. Cook the eggplant for about 5 minutes, then add the zucchini. Add the tomato next, along with the cinnamon, cumin, clove, and paprika. Add about ½ teaspoon of salt and stir to combine, cooking for another 7 to 10 minutes, or until the vegetables soften a bit but aren't fully cooked through. Add the kale and cook until wilted. Add the remaining 2 tablespoons (30 ml) oil and stir to combine. Check for seasoning and add more salt if necessary.

Lay out the slices of bread and divide the mixture evenly among 4 of the slices. Top each with other slices of bread.

FEATURED SUPERFOODS:
Cinnamon, cumin, garlic, kale, olive oil, onions, tomatoes, zucchini

MUSHROOM AND BEET GREEN PESTO SANDWICH

RECOMMENDED BREAD: Buckwheat Caraway Beet Bread,
Buttermilk Whole Wheat Bread, Parmesan Kale Bread

YIELD: 4 sandwiches

Beet greens pesto is a great addition to practically any sandwich but especially ones that feature earthy notes, like this portobello mushroom sandwich. The mushrooms, which absorb flavor well and have a natural meatiness to them, are an excellent match for the pesto, which adds texture as well as flavor, while the crumbled blue cheese provides a welcome tanginess. This sandwich is best paired with bread that has seeds in it, too, for added texture and heartiness.

3 portobello mushroom caps

½ teaspoon salt

8 slices bread

1 cup (260 g) Beet Greens and Pecan Pesto (page 44)

½ cup (75 g) crumbled blue cheese

Preheat the oven to 400°F (200°C, or gas mark 6). Clean the portobello caps by brushing off any dirt or quickly rinsing them. Using a spoon, scrape out the gills (the dark brown underside) of the mushrooms. Lay the mushrooms on a baking sheet and sprinkle with the salt. Bake until cooked through, about 15 minutes. Remove from the oven and set aside to cool. When they are cool enough to handle, thinly slice.

To assemble the sandwich, lay out the slices of bread. Divide up the pesto and slather it on the bread. Divide the mushroom slices among 4 slices of bread. Place equal amounts of the cheese on top of the mushrooms and top each sandwich with the second slice of bread.

FEATURED SUPERFOODS:
Beet greens, lemons, mushrooms, olive oil, pecans

WARM BEET GREEN PESTO
POTATO AND LEEK SALAD SANDWICH

RECOMMENDED BREAD: Sub rolls, baguette, Middle Eastern–Spiced Oat Flaxseed Buns

YIELD: 4 sandwiches

It doesn't get more American than potato salad, and this sandwich just begs to be taken outside for a picnic. It's best served warm or at room temperature, preferably on top of a checkered blanket or tablecloth, in the middle of a park on a warm summer day. This sandwich changes things up a bit with an earthy beet green pesto clinging to the roasted potatoes.

4 cups (440 g) diced potato, preferably red potatoes or Yukon gold

1 tablespoon plus 1 teaspoon (20 ml) olive oil, divided

1 teaspoon kosher salt, plus more to taste

¾ cup (75 g) diced leeks

1 cup (260 g) Beet Greens and Pecan Pesto (page 44)

4 sub rolls, sliced in half

Preheat the oven to 400°F (200°C, or gas mark 6) and line a baking sheet with parchment paper. Spread the potatoes on the prepared baking sheet. Coat them evenly with 1 tablespoon (15 ml) of the oil and sprinkle with the salt. Roast the potatoes until they start to brown and are soft all the way through, about 20 minutes. Note: You may need to turn the potatoes over with a spatula if they start to get too brown on one side. Remove from the oven and set aside to cool slightly.

Meanwhile, heat the remaining 1 teaspoon (5 ml) olive oil in a medium-size skillet over medium heat. Add the leeks and a pinch of salt. Sauté the leeks until they start to get translucent and soft, about 5 minutes.

In a large bowl, combine the roasted potatoes with the sautéed leeks. Add the pesto and stir to combine. Season to taste with salt.

Lay out the sub rolls and divide the potato-leek mixture among them.

FEATURED SUPERFOODS:
Beet greens, leeks, lemons, olive oil, pecans

BUFFALO BRUSSELS SPROUTS SUB WITH BLUE CHEESE, CARROT, AND CELERY SLAW

RECOMMENDED BREAD: Sub rolls (really, that's what this sandwich begs to be on)

YIELD: 4 subs

My husband and I have an obsession with all things buffalo sauced, and I think that, as odd as it may sound, buffalo sauce and Brussels sprouts are a great and underrated pairing because the sauce really gives the sprouts an added punch of flavor. To complement the buffalo sauce, this sandwich is then classically finished off with a tangy blue cheese, carrot, and celery slaw, which gives the palate a little relief from the sting of the sauce. We make versions of this sandwich, either with different vegetables or sometimes chicken too, especially during football season. The amount of sauce you use is up to you, and I recommend seeking out a sauce that is thick and labeled "buffalo sauce" and not just hot sauce. You'll get the best results that way.

1 pound (454 g) Brussels sprouts

2 tablespoons (30 ml) extra-virgin olive oil

Kosher salt, to taste

¾ cup (180 g) buffalo sauce, or to taste

1 medium-size carrot, peeled

1 stalk celery

½ cup (120 g) Greek yogurt

¼ cup (35 g) crumbled blue cheese

4 sub rolls, sliced in half and lightly toasted

Preheat the oven to 400°F (200°C, or gas mark 6) and line a baking sheet with parchment paper. Prepare the Brussels sprouts by washing them, trimming their stem ends off, and then halving them. Place them in a single layer on the prepared baking sheet. Drizzle with oil, rolling them to coat, and season with salt. Roast the Brussels sprouts until golden brown, 35 to 40 minutes. Remove from the oven, place in a bowl, add the buffalo sauce, turn to coat, and set aside until ready to assemble the sandwiches.

Meanwhile, prepare the slaw by cutting the carrot and celery in half and then cut each half into small, matchstick-size sticks. Place in a bowl, add the yogurt and cheese, and stir to combine.

To assemble, lay out the rolls and top each evenly with the buffalo Brussels sprouts and the slaw.

FEATURED SUPERFOODS:
Brussels sprouts, carrots, Greek yogurt, olive oil

SKINNY'S CRISPY KALE CHICKEN CAESAR SALAD SANDWICH

RECOMMENDED BREAD: Middle Eastern–Spiced Oat Flaxseed Buns,
Parmesan Kale Bread, rolls

YIELD: 4 sandwiches

I affectionately call my husband Skinny, which may seem like an odd nickname, but it's what his last name (and now mine, too) means in Polish, and it's part of how we named our company, the Skinny Beet. He makes one of the best Caesar salads around, and our clients request it regularly. He started making it with crispy kale for a change of pace. It's always a hit—and now you can make it, too. If you're unsure about using anchovies, I swear you won't know that they're in there, but if you really aren't into them, you can leave them out. Just don't tell Skinny.

¼ cup plus 1 teaspoon (65 ml) extra-virgin olive oil

1½ pounds (680 g) boneless, skinless chicken breast

1½ teaspoons kosher salt, divided

2 cups (140 g) kale, torn into large pieces

3 small cloves garlic, skins on

1 egg yolk

1 teaspoon Worcestershire sauce

1½ teaspoons lemon zest

½ teaspoon Dijon mustard

½ teaspoon anchovy paste

1 tablespoon (15 ml) fresh lemon juice

2 tablespoons (30 ml) grapeseed oil or other neutral-flavored oil

2 tablespoons (10 g) grated Parmesan cheese

4 buns, sliced in half

Preheat the oven to 375°F (190°C, or gas mark 5) and line a baking sheet with parchment paper. In a large ovenproof skillet, heat 1 teaspoon (5 ml) of the oil over medium-high heat. Season the chicken with 1 teaspoon of the salt and slide it into the hot skillet. Sear the chicken on each side, turning it only once, after it has developed a golden crust, 5 to 7 minutes. Transfer the skillet to the oven and cook the chicken through, about 10 to 15 minutes, or until it registers an internal temperature of 165°F (74°C). Remove from the oven and set aside to cool for at least 5 minutes before slicing into thin strips.

Meanwhile, place the kale on the prepared baking sheet and bake until crispy but still green, 10 to 12 minutes. Remove from the oven and set aside.

In a small skillet, combine the garlic with the remaining ¼ cup (60 ml) olive oil over medium heat, stirring regularly. Once the garlic has started to brown, 5 to 7 minutes, remove from the heat and set aside to cool. Reserve the oil. Once cool, peel the skin from the garlic and put into a food processor. Add the egg yolk, Worcestershire sauce, lemon zest, mustard, anchovy paste, and lemon juice and process. Mix the reserved oil with the grapeseed oil. Slowly pour the oil into the processor and then add the cheese. The mixture can be thick, which makes for a good coating, but if you want it a little thinner, you can stream in some water. Season with the remaining ½ teaspoon salt.

To assemble the sandwiches, lay out the buns. Spread the Caesar dressing inside the buns. Divide up the chicken and add to the bottom part of each bun. Divide up the kale and place on top of the chicken. Place the top half of the bun on top of the kale.

FEATURED SUPERFOODS:

Eggs, garlic, kale, lemons, olive oil

ARGENTINIAN STEAK SANDWICH
WITH KALE CHIMICHURRI

RECOMMENDED BREAD: Parmesan Kale Bread, Buttermilk Whole Wheat Bread, rolls

YIELD: 4 sandwiches

Chimichurri sauce is a classic Argentinian condiment that is commonly used on top of steak. It's very easy to put together, and its purpose is to be pungent and loud, letting its herby, vinegary, garlicky presence be known. (It also goes fantastically on some warm, roasted potatoes, by the way.) I've added kale to this blend of herbs, giving it more texture and an earthier flavor. It's paired traditionally in this sandwich with steak—simple and extremely satisfying. It also goes well with fish, if you want an alternative to steak.

⅓ cup (22 g) minced kale

¼ cup (4 g) minced cilantro

½ teaspoon minced garlic

Pinch of red pepper flakes, to taste (optional)

2 tablespoons (30 ml) red wine vinegar

2 tablespoons (30 ml) extra-virgin olive oil

Salt

1½ pounds (680 g) skirt steak

2 tablespoons (30 ml) grapeseed oil

¼ teaspoon black pepper

8 slices bread

In a medium-size bowl, combine the kale, cilantro, and garlic. Stir to combine and add the pepper flakes, if using, along with the vinegar and olive oil. Stir to combine and add a pinch of salt to taste. Set aside until ready to use.

Trim the steak of visible and large chunks of fat. Heat the grapeseed oil in a large skillet over medium-high heat for about 3 minutes. Sprinkle the steak with salt and pepper. Add the steak to the hot oil and cook for about 3 minutes, flipping it and cooking for another 3 minutes or so until the desired doneness. Remove from the heat and set aside to rest for at least 5 to 7 minutes.

Once the steak has rested, cut it into thin slices. Lay out the bread and top 4 slices with the steak. Finish by adding the kale chimichurri sauce and the last slices of bread.

FEATURED SUPERFOODS:
Cilantro, garlic, kale, olive oil

CARAMELIZED ENDIVE AND FENNEL SANDWICH WITH GORGONZOLA DOLCE

RECOMMENDED BREAD: Buckwheat Caraway Beet Bread,
Buttermilk Whole Wheat Bread, whole wheat bread

YIELD: 4 sandwiches

There's always been a great debate in our house on the pronunciation of the word *endive*. My husband likes to say it just as it's spelled: EN-dive. I like to say it the fancier way, pronouncing it on-DEEVE, making it sound like an exotic and luxurious ingredient. No matter which way you say it, endive is a nutritious ingredient. When you roast it, it becomes soft and caramelized, which is a natural match for Gorgonzola dolce, a less potent and slightly sweeter version of Gorgonzola cheese. Fennel gives this sandwich additional nutrition and texture as well as a light anise flavor. I always like to reserve the fennel fronds, those wispy green bits at the top, for garnish.

2 endives

1 fennel bulb

2 tablespoons (30 ml) extra-virgin olive oil

½ teaspoon kosher salt

2 ounces (56 g) Gorgonzola dolce

8 slices bread

Preheat the oven to 400°F (200°C, or gas mark 6) and line a baking sheet with parchment paper. Cut the endives in half lengthwise and place on one side of the prepared baking sheet. Using only the white bulb part of the fennel, remove the core of the fennel with a knife and thinly slice the fennel. Reserve the green fronds for later. Lay the fennel slices in a single layer on the other side of the baking sheet. Drizzle the oil and sprinkle the salt evenly over all the vegetables. Roast the vegetables until they start to caramelize and turn brown, 25 to 30 minutes. Remove from the oven. Break up the Gorgonzola dolce and crumble it over the endive.

To assemble, lay out the slices of bread. Top 4 of them with one of the endive pieces (you may need to cut them in half and stack them to make it fit better). Divide up the fennel and add on top of each endive piece. Finish by placing the other slice of bread on top.

FEATURED SUPERFOOD:
Olive oil

Chapter 5

SUPERFOOD SPOTLIGHT:
Vegetables

MUSHROOM AND CANDIED WALNUT BAKED BRIE SANDWICH

RECOMMENDED BREAD: Buttermilk Whole Wheat Bread, Spelt and Flaxseed Challah, wheat or oat bread

YIELD: 4 sandwiches

Baked Brie is a marvelous cheese, especially melted and gooey and topped with fruity compotes or candied nuts. This sandwich mimics these flavors and qualities that make baked Brie so satisfying and adds hearty portobello mushrooms and candied walnuts. This recipe makes extra candied walnuts than you'll need for the sandwich, but you'll thank me for it later. It's impossible not to enjoy snacking on them.

4 portobello mushroom caps

2 teaspoons extra-virgin olive oil

Kosher salt, to taste

1½ cups (225 g) walnuts

1 tablespoon (14 g) unsalted butter

1 teaspoon ground cinnamon

2 teaspoons brown sugar

1 teaspoon chopped fresh rosemary

8 slices bread

4 tablespoons (44 g) whole-grain mustard

12 ounces (336 g) Brie, thinly sliced

Preheat the oven to 400°F (200°C, or gas mark 6), or use a toaster oven. Scrub the mushroom caps thoroughly and using a spoon, scrape out the mushroom gills (the brown part underneath the cap). Slice the mushrooms into thin strips. Heat the oil in a large skillet and add the sliced mushrooms. Cook until they soften and brown, about 10 minutes. Add a generous pinch of salt, stir to combine, and remove from the heat.

Meanwhile, in a small skillet, combine the walnuts, butter, a pinch of salt, the cinnamon, brown sugar, and rosemary. Cook over medium heat, stirring occasionally; if the nuts start to brown too fast and irregularly, lower the heat a bit. Toast the nuts until they are an even shade of brown.

Lay out the bread and spread ½ tablespoon (5.5 g) of mustard onto each slice of bread. Add a little Brie to each slice and toast, either in the oven or in a toaster oven, until the cheese melts. Divide the mushrooms evenly among the slices of bread and top with the candied walnuts. Press the 2 halves together and enjoy while warm.

FEATURED SUPERFOODS:
Cinnamon, mushrooms, olive oil, rosemary, walnuts

EDAMAME PEA SANDWICH WITH LEMON PEPPER RICOTTA

RECOMMENDED BREAD: Honey Miso Whole Wheat Sesame Buns, Spelt and Flaxseed Challah, whole wheat bread

YIELD: 4 sandwiches

This sandwich is so easy to throw together at a moment's notice or on the fly. I usually keep bags of frozen peas and edamame, just for something like this. I find that I crave this sandwich in the early spring when I want something light after a winter of eating heavier, heartier dishes. If I have the extra time, I'll shuck fresh peas and swap those out for frozen, but because they're only in season for a short period of time and this sandwich is meant to be something that you can throw together quickly, frozen is just fine.

1 cup (250 g) ricotta cheese

1 tablespoon (6 g) lemon zest

1 teaspoon lemon juice

Kosher salt, to taste

Black pepper, to taste

1 teaspoon honey

8 slices bread

½ cup (75 g) frozen peas, defrosted

½ cup (75 g) frozen edamame, defrosted

8 mint leaves

8 basil leaves

In a small bowl, combine the ricotta cheese with the lemon zest and lemon juice and season with salt. Add the pepper and drizzle in the honey. Set aside.

Lay out the bread on a work surface. Spread each slice with 2 tablespoons (30 g) of the ricotta cheese mixture. Divide the peas and edamame among 4 slices of bread. Last, divide the mint and basil evenly among the sandwiches and top with the remaining bread.

FEATURED SUPERFOODS:
Basil, edamame, honey, lemons, mint

BEET AND GOAT CHEESE PIE SANDWICH

RECOMMENDED BREAD: Middle Eastern–Spiced Oat Flaxseed Buns,
Buckwheat Caraway Beet Bread, Parmesan Kale Bread, Semolina Quinoa Focaccia

YIELD: 4 sandwiches

This pie is similar to hash browns but made with shredded beets and pears. It is dotted with goat cheese and cooked with rice flour to help give it a crispy finish. Once it comes out of the oven, it's easy to cut and acts like a veggie "burger" in that sense. If you're discouraged by beets, try it with sweet potatoes, white potatoes, or a blend of both. Or you can try gradually introducing beets into the mix by using half potato and half beet.

1½ cups (180 g) shredded beets

½ cup (60 g) shredded pear

¼ cup (30 g) flaxseed meal

¼ cup (30 g) rice flour

Kosher salt

1 egg

4 ounces (112 g) goat cheese

4 buns, sliced in half

1 cup (30 g) watercress

Preheat the oven to 425°F (220°C, or gas mark 7) and line a baking sheet with parchment paper. In a large bowl, combine the beets, pear, flaxseed meal, and rice flour. (I strongly advise that you wear gloves, or your hands will temporarily be dyed hot pink!) Using your hands, toss all of the ingredients together and season with salt. Add the egg and combine well. Spread the beet-pear mixture onto the prepared baking sheet. Make a nice even square (about 6 x 6 inches, or 15 x 15 cm) using about half of the total mixture. Break the goat cheese up with your hands and dot the surface of the beet cake with it. Cover the goat cheese with the remaining beet mixture and flatten out into one large cake. Bake for 20 to 25 minutes, until the edges get crispy and brown a bit. Remove from the oven and set aside to cool slightly.

To assemble, lay out the buns and divide the watercress among the sandwiches. Cut the beet cake into 4 pieces and place on top of the watercress. Top each sandwich with the top part of the bun.

FEATURED SUPERFOODS:
Beets, eggs, flaxseeds, watercress

VEGETARIAN CUBAN SANDWICH

RECOMMENDED BREAD: French bread, sub rolls, baguette

YIELD: 4 sandwiches

One of my all-time favorite sandwiches is the Cuban—a mix of marinated pork, Swiss cheese, mustard, pickles, and sometimes ham or salami that gets pressed between French bread. This is a vegetarian version with a lot of the same components that make this sandwich so great. Play around with it by adding different vegetables to the mix to further change things up or just to use up what you have on hand. You can make this without the cheese for a vegan meal and still get great results, or you could slip a couple of pieces of prosciutto in there for good measure.

3 large portobello mushroom caps

1 tablespoon (15 ml) olive oil

1½ cups (180 g) sliced zucchini (about 2 medium or 1 large zucchini)

¼ teaspoon kosher salt

1 avocado

2 tablespoons (30 ml) lime juice

4 sub roll–size pieces of French bread

¼ cup (44 g) Dijon mustard

1 cup (120 g) sliced kosher pickles

8 slices tomato

4 slices Swiss cheese

Preheat the oven to 400°F (200°C, or gas mark 6). Scrub the portobello mushroom caps well to remove all dirt. Cut out the stems and using a spoon, scoop out the dark brown gills on the underside. Slice the mushrooms into thin, ½-inch (1.3 cm) strips. In a large skillet, heat the oil over medium heat for about 1 minute. Add the mushrooms to the oil and cook for 2 to 3 minutes, until they start to give off water. Add the zucchini and salt and sauté until the vegetables are cooked through, 5 to 7 minutes.

Cut the avocado in half lengthwise and remove the pit with a knife. Scoop out the flesh and cut into thin strips. Marinate the avocado in lime juice to prevent browning.

To assemble the sandwiches, lay out the piece of bread. Spread the mustard on the bottom halves of each sub roll. Layer each roll with the cooked zucchini and mushrooms and follow with the avocado and pickles. Top with 2 slices of tomato and 1 slice of cheese and then the top of the roll. Place the sandwiches on a baking sheet, and then place a piece of foil on top of each sandwich. Place another baking sheet on top of the foil, and then add something ovenproof and heavy to press the sandwiches together (a heavy skillet or pot work well). Bake the sandwiches until the cheese melts and the bread is toasted, 5 to 7 minutes. Remove from the oven.

FEATURED SUPERFOODS:
Avocados, limes, mushrooms, olive oil, tomatoes, zucchini

MOLE-RUBBED CAULIFLOWER SANDWICH

RECOMMENDED BREAD: Sub rolls, Cornmeal Texas Toast

YIELD: 4 sandwiches

Mole is a popular Mexican sauce made of spices and nuts simmered for hours on end. While the components of the sauce vary, the ingredient that is constant is cocoa, which gives it its deep flavor and dark color. This is a great vegetarian option that is easy to pull together for a hearty weeknight meal, much easier than making mole from scratch, but still getting some of those great flavors. Spicy, smoky, and packed with bright and tangy flavors, it is great warm or at room temperature. To make it vegan, just omit the cheese.

1 head cauliflower

1½ teaspoons ground cumin

1 teaspoon ground coriander

1 teaspoon smoked paprika

½ teaspoon ground cinnamon

1½ teaspoons unsweetened cocoa powder

Olive oil

Kosher salt, to taste

4 slices smoked Cheddar cheese

4 sub rolls

1 cup (240 g) Chipotle Black Bean Spread (page 39)

Tomatillo Yogurt Sauce (page 41)

Fresh cilantro sprigs

Wash the cauliflower and remove the green stems. Cut the cauliflower into thick pieces. In a large, nonstick skillet, combine the cumin, coriander, paprika, cinnamon, and cocoa powder. Dry toast the spices over medium heat just until they become fragrant and you can begin to see little wisps of smoke. (This happens fast, so be sure to keep an eye on them.) Let the spices cool a bit, and then use your hands to rub the spice blend thoroughly over the cauliflower slices.

In the same large skillet, heat just enough oil to lightly coat the bottom of the skillet, and then add the cauliflower. Season both sides generously with salt, and cook over medium heat, turning regularly to ensure even cooking, until the cauliflower has softened and is cooked through, 10 to 15 minutes. Remove from the heat. Place the cheese over the cauliflower and put a lid on the skillet to melt the cheese.

Meanwhile, slice the rolls lengthwise and lightly toast. To assemble the sandwich, spread ¼ cup (60 g) of the black bean spread on each of the bottom pieces. Spread ¼ cup (60 g) of the tomatillo yogurt sauce on each of the top pieces. Place the cauliflower with the melted cheese on top of the black bean spread and garnish with cilantro. Top the sandwich with the other half of the roll. Enjoy immediately or wrap to enjoy later that day.

FEATURED SUPERFOODS:
Beans, cauliflower, cilantro, cinnamon, cocoa, cumin, Greek yogurt, limes, olive oil, peppers

SWEET POTATO, PEAR, AND PROSCIUTTO SANDWICH

RECOMMENDED BREAD: Cayenne Maple Sweet Potato Biscuits, Semolina Quinoa Focaccia, Parmesan Kale Bread

YIELD: 4 sandwiches

This sandwich makes for a great break from the normal breakfast or brunch. It's got that perfect storm of salty-sweet that I love so much, and it's a great fit for a savory breakfast. Of course, it's ideal for other meals, too, but there's something about this sandwich that makes me think if I start my day with it, then I'm off to a great start. If you wanted to get real cute, you could make miniature versions of these sandwiches and serve them as sliders at a party. They'd be a hit!

2 medium-size sweet potatoes

1 tablespoon (15 ml) olive oil

1 teaspoon kosher salt

4 biscuits

4 tablespoons (44 g) grainy mustard

4 slices sharp Cheddar cheese

4 slices prosciutto

Preheat the oven to 400°F (200°C, or gas mark 6) or use a toaster oven, and line a baking sheet with parchment paper. Scrub the sweet potatoes, peel them, cut them into 1-inch rounds, coat evenly with oil, and sprinkle with salt. Place on the baking sheet. Roast the sweet potatoes until they turn golden and soften, 25 to 30 minutes. Set aside until ready to use.

Meanwhile, slice the biscuits in half lengthwise. Slather 1 tablespoon (11 g) mustard on each biscuit, coating both halves, and layer on 1 slice of cheese. Place on a baking sheet and toast the biscuits either in the oven or a toaster oven, just until the cheese melts. Divide the sweet potatoes among the biscuits and top each sandwich with a slice of prosciutto.

FEATURED SUPERFOODS:
Olive oil, sweet potatoes

INDIAN MUSHROOM AND CHICKPEA FLOUR VEGGIE BURGERS WITH CURRIED YOGURT SAUCE

RECOMMENDED BREAD: Sub rolls, burger buns,
Middle Eastern–Spiced Oat Flaxseed Buns

YIELD: 4 veggie burgers

Much to my husband's chagrin, I love veggie burgers. They are surprisingly simple to make, and their versatility is limitless. The best secret to making a good one that's not mushy is to use chickpea flour, sometimes called garbanzo flour. It gives them a crispness that is tough to achieve otherwise. They're also super healthy and loaded with protein, fiber, and iron.

SANDWICH

1 tablespoon (15 ml) extra-virgin olive oil, plus some for the pan

1 cup (70 g) roughly chopped cremini mushrooms

½ teaspoon kosher salt, divided

1¼ cups (150 g) chickpea flour

1 teaspoon curry powder

½ cup (75 g) frozen peas, thawed

2 tablespoons (2 g) chopped cilantro

Water, at room temperature

4 burger buns, sliced in half

1 cup (30 g) fresh baby spinach

Curried Yogurt Sauce (page 99)

To make the sandwich: In a small skillet, heat the oil over medium heat and add the mushrooms. Once the mushrooms start to brown a bit, add ¼ teaspoon of the salt and cook until softened and deep brown in color, about 15 minutes. Transfer to a bowl and set aside to cool.

In a medium-size bowl, combine the flour, curry powder, peas, cilantro, and cooked mushrooms. Slowly pour in room-temperature water in a steady stream while stirring. Continue adding the water, ¼ cup (60 ml) at a time, and stirring, just until a thick batter forms, resembling cookie dough.

In a medium-size ovenproof skillet over medium-high heat, add just enough oil to lightly coat the skillet and heat for a minute or two. Divide the veggie burger mix into 4 equal portions and shape them with a spoon, then slide them into the hot oil. Cook for about 3 minutes on each side. Place the skillet into the oven to cook the inside, about 5 minutes.

Meanwhile, toast the buns if you'd like. Lay out the buns, divide the spinach among them, and place a veggie burger on top. Top each burger with 1 tablespoon (15 g) of the curried yogurt sauce.

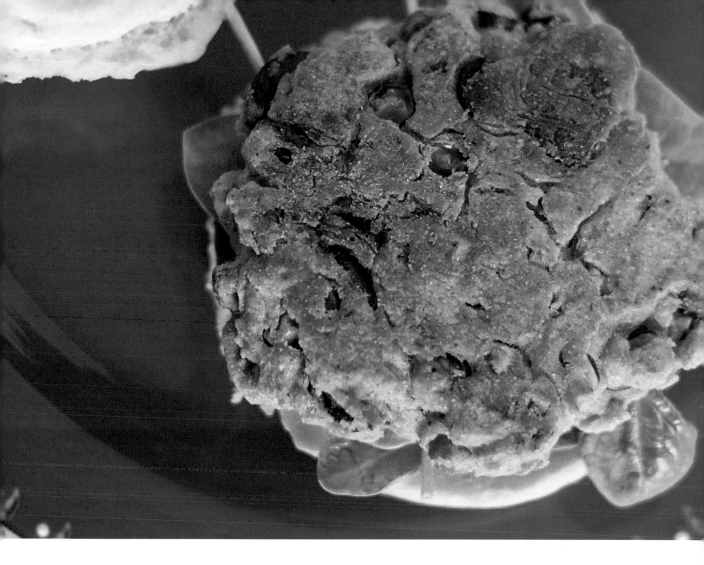

CURRIED YOGURT SAUCE

¼ cup (60 g) Greek yogurt

¼ teaspoon lime zest

¼ teaspoon curry powder

To make the curried yogurt sauce: Combine all of the ingredients in a small bowl and blend with a spoon. Set aside until ready to use

FEATURED SUPERFOODS:

Chickpea flour, cilantro, Greek yogurt, limes, mushrooms, olive oil, spinach

ROASTED RED PEPPER AND CAULIFLOWER SANDWICH

RECOMMENDED BREAD: Parmesan Kale Bread, Middle Eastern–Spiced Oat Flaxseed Buns, sub rolls

YIELD: 4 sandwiches

Roasting cauliflower is a completely different experience than boiling or sautéing it. It's even easier to prepare because it's very hands-off; just let the oven do the work. Roasted cauliflower develops this gorgeous, deep brown color that only intensifies its flavor. In this sandwich, it gets paired with the Smoky and Spicy Red Pepper Pesto, which enhances the cauliflower's natural nuttiness and adds just a hint of spice and heat.

4 cups (400 g) chopped cauliflower (about 1 small head)

2 tablespoons (30 g) extra-virgin olive oil

1 teaspoon kosher salt

2 red bell peppers

8 slices bread

1 cup (240 g) Smoky and Spicy Red Pepper Pesto (page 38)

1 cup (30 g) spinach

Preheat the oven to 400°F (200°C, or gas mark 6) and line a baking sheet with parchment paper. In a bowl, coat the cauliflower in the oil and spread in an even layer on the prepared baking sheet. Sprinkle with the salt. Roast the cauliflower until it softens and the edges start to brown, 30 to 40 minutes. Set aside until ready to use.

Meanwhile, line a small baking sheet with parchment paper and add the red bell peppers. Roast the peppers until they blacken, turning every so often to ensure even roasting. Once they are evenly blackened, 20 to 30 minutes, transfer to a bowl and cover with plastic wrap, allowing the steam to help separate the skin. Let sit until cool enough to handle, 5 to 10 minutes. Once you can comfortably hold the peppers, peel the skin away and remove the stem and seeds. Don't worry about getting all of the black char off; leaving some behind adds a smoky flavor. Slice into long strips and season with a pinch of salt.

To assemble, lay out the bread. Spread the pesto evenly over all of the slices of bread. Divide the spinach among 4 slices of bread and lay the roasted red pepper strips down on top of the spinach. Divide the cauliflower equally among the sandwiches and top with the remaining bread.

FEATURED SUPERFOODS:
Cauliflower, chives, cilantro, hazelnuts, lemons, olive oil, pecans, peppers, spinach

SAGE-ROASTED PUMPKIN AND SMOKED GOUDA MELT

RECOMMENDED BREAD: Spelt and Flaxseed Challah, Buttermilk Whole Wheat Bread, Parmesan Kale Bread, Cayenne Maple Sweet Potato Biscuits, oat or whole wheat bread

YIELD: 4 sandwiches

Perfect for fueling my grilled cheese obsession, this sandwich is great to make in the fall when pumpkins are in season and widely available. Roasting a pumpkin is easy to do, and the results are far better than anything in a can. It has the same heartiness that sweet potatoes have but a different flavor altogether. That said, if you are craving this when pumpkin is out of season or you just don't have the time to roast a pumpkin, you can use pumpkin purée from a can. Just add a pinch of ground cloves, 2 or 3 chopped sage leaves, and salt. You may also want to sweeten it a bit as well with some honey or maple syrup and spread it over the sandwiches before you add the cheese.

1 (1½- to 2-pound, or 680 to 908 g) sugar pumpkin

8 sage leaves

8 whole cloves

2 teaspoons salt

8 slices bread

4 slices smoked Gouda cheese

¼ cup (35 g) pumpkin seeds

Preheat the oven to 400°F (200°C, or gas mark 6) and line a baking sheet with parchment paper. Cut the pumpkin into thin slices. (This can be dangerous because the pumpkin can be slippery, so be careful! I find it helps to start dividing the pumpkin into fourths and then eighths and so on until you get the desired size.) Scoop out the seeds. Lay the sage leaves on the fleshy side of the pumpkin and pierce each sage leaf with a clove. Sprinkle evenly with salt. Transfer the pumpkin pieces to the prepared baking sheet and roast until very soft, 35 to 40 minutes. Set aside until cool enough to handle. At this point, the outer skin should slide right off. Discard it.

To assemble the sandwiches, lay out the bread and top 4 of the slices with equal amounts of pumpkin slices and 1 slice of cheese. Sprinkle with the pumpkin seeds and top each with the remaining slice of bread. Place the sandwiches on the baking sheet and bake until the bread is toasted and the cheese has melted, 7 to 10 minutes.

FEATURED SUPERFOODS:
Pumpkin/pumpkin seeds, sage

CURRIED BROCCOLI SANDWICH WITH TOASTED CASHEWS

RECOMMENDED BREAD: Sub rolls, Honey Miso Whole Wheat Sesame Buns

YIELD: 4 sandwiches

When you coat broccoli in curried yogurt and then broil it, something amazing happens. The bright yellow yogurt clings to the broccoli and creates a crust that looks just as great as it tastes. Toasting cashews, just like when you toast any nut, releases their oils, enhances their flavor, and allows them to really shine.

½ cup (75 g) unsalted cashews

1 cup (240 g) Greek yogurt

2 teaspoons curry powder

¼ teaspoon turmeric

4 cups (280 g) broccoli florets

½ teaspoon kosher salt

4 sub rolls, sliced in half

¼ cup (4 g) roughly chopped cilantro

Preheat the oven to 400°F (200°C, or gas mark 6). Lay the cashews in a single layer on a baking sheet. Roast the nuts until they turn a deep golden brown, 7 to 10 minutes. Remove from the oven and set aside to cool.

In a medium-size bowl, combine the yogurt with the curry powder and turmeric. Add the broccoli to the bowl and stir to combine, coating the broccoli in the yogurt. Lay the broccoli in a single layer on a baking sheet, sprinkle with the salt, place on the top rack in the oven, and change the oven temperature to broil. Cook the broccoli until it starts to get very dark in color, about 5 minutes. Remove from the oven and stir the broccoli. Return to the oven and cook for a couple minutes more, until the broccoli is done. Set aside to cool.

To assemble the sandwiches, lay out the sub rolls. Divide the broccoli among 4 slices and top with the toasted cashews. Sprinkle the cilantro on each sandwich and top with the remaining sub rolls.

FEATURED SUPERFOODS:
Broccoli, cashews, cilantro, Greek yogurt, turmeric

SWEET POTATO "FALAFEL" SANDWICH

RECOMMENDED BREAD: Middle Eastern–Spiced Oat Flaxseed Buns

YIELD: 4 sandwiches

Ever since my introduction to falafel, I've been trying to make different versions of this much-loved Middle Eastern fritter. A fun play off of it, this recipe relies on sweet potatoes instead of chickpeas as a base. I use familiar and traditional falafel spices and herbs, which keeps it similar but results in something very different. Because these falafel aren't fried, they can be softer than a regular falafel, but adding cucumber to the sandwich helps give it crunch.

2 cups (220 g) diced sweet potato

1 tablespoon (15 ml) olive oil

½ teaspoon kosher salt

1 teaspoon ground cumin

2 tablespoons (12 g) chopped scallion

¼ cup (4 g) fresh cilantro, plus more for garnish

1 teaspoon minced garlic

1 tablespoon (15 ml) lemon juice

½ to ¾ cup (60 to 90 g) chickpea flour, divided

4 buns

¾ cup (180 g) Greek yogurt

Sliced cucumber, for garnish

Preheat the oven to 375°F (190°C, or gas mark 5). Line a baking sheet with parchment paper. Coat the sweet potatoes with the oil and salt in a small bowl and lay on the baking sheet. Roast until the potatoes are soft and light brown, 25 to 30 minutes, then cool slightly.

Add the sweet potatoes, cumin, scallion, cilantro, garlic, lemon juice, and ½ cup (60 g) of the chickpea flour to a food processor and coarsely chop until it begins to come together. It should look like cookie batter. If it does not hold its shape, add the remaining ¼ cup (30 g) flour. Form the dough into balls a little smaller than a golf ball. Place on the baking sheet and bake until they start to brown a little, flipping them halfway, if needed, 20 to 30 minutes.

Meanwhile, split the buns in half and toast until warm, 3 to 5 minutes. Spread the buns with the yogurt. Add a couple of the falafel balls to each bun, and garnish with the cilantro and cucumber.

FEATURED SUPERFOODS:
Chickpea flour, cilantro, cumin, garlic, Greek yogurt, lemons, olive oil, sweet potatoes

ASIAN SLOPPY JOE SANDWICH

RECOMMENDED BREAD: Honey Miso Whole Wheat Sesame Buns,
whole wheat buns, burger buns

YIELD: 4 sandwiches

A version of this recipe was created one night when we bought a bunch of produce and had some friends over. We had no plan other than to cook and create. We sipped wine while the direction of the meal moved toward sandwiches. One person chopped, another made the bread, one took care of cooking it all, and the other made sure our wine glasses were filled, and that's how this sandwich was born. Although this is a vegetarian sandwich, if you wanted to add some ground meat, I'm sure no one would stop you.

½ teaspoon coconut oil

¼ cup (40 g) diced shallot

2 teaspoons minced garlic

3 cups (210 g) sliced shiitake mushrooms

6 cups (492 g) cubed eggplant (about 1 medium-size eggplant)

2 tablespoons (30 ml) soy sauce, more to taste

2 teaspoons nam pla (fish sauce)

1½ teaspoons grated fresh ginger

2 teaspoons ponzu sauce or lime juice

Sriracha, to taste (optional)

2 tablespoons (2 g) chopped fresh cilantro

4 buns or rolls, sliced in half

Heat the oil in a large skillet over medium heat for about a minute. Add the shallot and sauté for a couple of minutes, just until they soften. Add the garlic and cook for another minute. Add the mushrooms and sauté until they soften and start to brown, 7 to 10 minutes. Add the eggplant, soy sauce, fish sauce, and ginger. Stir to combine and let cook until the eggplant becomes very soft, 15 to 20 minutes. Add the ponzu sauce, sriracha (if using), and cilantro. Season to taste with soy sauce. Divide the mixture evenly among the 4 buns.

FEATURED SUPERFOODS:
Cilantro, coconut oil, garlic, ginger, limes, mushrooms

SWEET POTATO POUTINE SANDWICH WITH MUSHROOM GRAVY

RECOMMENDED BREAD: Sub rolls

YIELD: 4 sandwiches

Poutine is not something that you'd expect to find in a book of this sort, and that's exactly why I wanted it in here. My husband's family is Canadian, and when we travel up north to visit them, it's rare that we don't have poutine—that illustrious Canadian classic that combines fries, gravy, and cheese curds. If you haven't had it before, it's a total guilty pleasure. This is a slimmed-down and much healthier take, served up via a sandwich.

1 large sweet potato, washed, peeled, and cut lengthwise into thin sticks

2 tablespoons (30 ml) extra-virgin olive oil, divided

Kosher salt, to taste

1 tablespoon (1.7 g) minced fresh rosemary

½ teaspoon chopped garlic

2 cups (140 g) quartered cremini mushrooms

1 cup (235 ml) milk

4 sub rolls, sliced in half

¾ cup (90 g) cheese curds or small diced Cheddar cheese

Preheat the oven to 400°F (200°C, or gas mark 6) and line a baking sheet with parchment paper. In a large bowl, coat the sweet potatoes with 1 tablespoon (15 ml) of the oil and sprinkle generously with salt. Spread on the prepared baking sheet and roast, turning them over halfway through the cooking process, for 30 to 40 minutes, or until the potatoes have browned around the edges and are cooked through.

Meanwhile, heat the remaining 1 tablespoon (15 ml) oil in a medium-size skillet over medium heat. Add the rosemary and garlic and cook until the garlic softens and the rosemary becomes fragrant, about 2 minutes. Add the mushrooms and cook until softened and browned, about 15 minutes. Using a blender, purée three-fourths of the mushroom mixture with the milk. Season to taste with salt. Return the milk-mushroom mixture to the skillet with the remaining one-fourth of the mushrooms and warm gently over low heat.

To prepare the sandwiches, lightly toast the sub rolls in a toaster oven. Divide the sweet potatoes equally among the sub rolls and top with the mushroom gravy. Top each sandwich with equal amounts of cheese.

FEATURED SUPERFOODS:
Garlic, mushrooms, olive oil, rosemary, sweet potatoes

SWEET POTATO "STEAK" AND AVOCADO SANDWICH WITH RED ONION CRANBERRY TARRAGON JAM

RECOMMENDED BREAD: Spelt and Flaxseed Challah, Buttermilk Whole Wheat Bread, Middle Eastern–Spiced Oat Flaxseed Buns, whole wheat rolls

YIELD: 4 sandwiches

I'll admit, it seems silly to draw a parallel between a steak and a sweet potato, but in this sandwich, the heartiness of the roasted sweet potato rounds are almost steak-like and a great vegetarian option. Avocado, which tends to be a meatier fruit, adds another layer, and the Red Onion Cranberry Tarragon Jam sweetens the mix and ties it all together.

2 small sweet potatoes

2 tablespoons (30 ml) extra-virgin olive oil

1 teaspoon kosher salt

1 avocado

Juice of 1 lemon

8 slices bread, toasted

¾ cup (180 g) Red Onion Cranberry Tarragon Jam (page 35)

Microgreens or cilantro, for garnish

Preheat the oven to 400°F (200°C, or gas mark 6) and line a baking sheet with parchment paper. Scrub the sweet potatoes and peel them. Cut into ½-inch (1.3 cm) thick rounds and place on the prepared baking sheet. Drizzle with the oil and sprinkle with the salt. Roast the potatoes until they develop a golden brown exterior and are cooked through, about 30 minutes. Remove from the oven and set aside.

Cut the avocado in half lengthwise, working around the pit. Pull apart each half and, using a knife, remove the pit by carefully running the knife into it and then twisting the knife. (The pit should just pop out.) Immediately squeeze lemon juice all over the avocado to prevent discoloration. Scoop out the flesh with a spoon and thinly slice the avocado. Apply more lemon juice to the avocado, making sure to coat it completely.

Lay out the bread on a work surface. Spread the Red Onion Cranberry Tarragon Jam on 4 slices of bread. Divide the sweet potato slices evenly among the other 4 slices. Top with a layer of avocado and finish with microgreens or cilantro. Place the jam-covered bread on top.

FEATURED SUPERFOODS:
Avocados, cranberries, garlic, lemons, microgreens, olive oil, onions, sweet potatoes, tarragon

ROASTED ITALIAN BROCCOLI SANDWICH

RECOMMENDED BREAD: Sub rolls, burger buns

YIELD: 4 sandwiches

I've always been drawn to Italian food, culture, and the language. My husband and I went to Italy on our honeymoon, and I wanted to make a sandwich that was inspired by that trip and the addictive ricotta cheese that I couldn't get enough of while there. The colors of this sandwich are bright and vibrant, and they also just so happen to be the colors of the Italian flag. Roasting the broccoli unlocks a deep flavor and subtle crunch, and the creamy ricotta that gets mixed with lemon zest and spicy red pepper flakes gives this sandwich even more personality. Seek out the best-quality ricotta cheese you can find. It's worth it, I promise.

4 cups (280 g) broccoli florets

2 cups (350 g) grape tomatoes

1 tablespoon (15 ml) olive oil

1 teaspoon kosher salt

¾ cup (180 g) ricotta cheese

2 teaspoons lemon zest

1 tablespoon (2.5 g) chopped fresh basil

Crushed red pepper flakes, to taste

4 sub rolls, sliced in half

Preheat the oven to 400°F (200°C, or gas mark 6). Line a baking sheet with parchment paper and add the broccoli and grape tomatoes. Drizzle with the oil and toss with your fingers to combine. Sprinkle with the salt. Roast until the broccoli turns bright green and has some dark spots and the tomatoes have shrunken in size, 15 to 20 minutes.

Meanwhile, combine the ricotta cheese, lemon zest, basil, and red pepper flakes in a small bowl.

To assemble, lay out the sub rolls and divide the ricotta cheese mixture among the sandwiches. Top with the roasted tomatoes and broccoli and the top parts of the buns.

FEATURED SUPERFOODS:
Basil, broccoli, lemons, olive oil, tomatoes

Chapter 6

SUPERFOOD SPOTLIGHT:
Legumes

MISO CARROT SALAD SANDWICH

RECOMMENDED BREAD: Honey Miso Whole Wheat Sesame Buns, sub rolls, burger buns

YIELD: 4 sandwiches

This sandwich is for nights when taking more than 10 to 15 minutes to put together a meal isn't in the cards. It's also perfect for road trips and take-to-work lunches because it's so easy to transport and its bright, fresh flavors are the perfect pick-me-up for a midday slump.

2½ teaspoons white miso

2 tablespoons (30 ml) rice wine vinegar

½ teaspoon grated fresh ginger

2 tablespoons (2 g) chopped fresh cilantro

1 tablespoon (3 g) chopped fresh mint

1 teaspoon sesame seeds

3 cups (330 g) shredded carrot

1 cup (150 g) mandarin orange slices

4 buns, sliced in half

In a medium-size bowl, combine the white miso, rice wine vinegar, ginger, cilantro, mint, and sesame seeds. Add the carrots and stir to combine, making sure the miso vinaigrette coats the carrots evenly. Add the mandarin orange slices and stir to combine. Divide the carrot salad among the 4 buns.

FEATURED SUPERFOODS:
Carrots, cilantro, ginger, mint, miso, oranges, sesame seeds

EGGPLANT WALNUT "MEATLOAF" SANDWICH

RECOMMENDED BREAD: Semolina Quinoa Focaccia, Parmesan Kale Bread,
Middle Eastern–Spiced Oat Flaxseed Buns,
Buttermilk Whole Wheat Bread, Cayenne Maple Sweet Potato Biscuits

YIELD: 4 sandwiches

Mimicking a meatloaf but entirely vegetarian, this loaf is so satisfying and "meaty" from the nuts and roasted eggplant that chances are, you might not even miss the actual meat.

4 cups (320 g) large-diced eggplant (about 1 medium-size eggplant)

2 tablespoons (30 ml) extra-virgin olive oil

½ teaspoon kosher salt

1 cup (150 g) walnuts

⅓ cup (35 g) grated Parmesan cheese

1 large egg

¼ cup (10 g) fresh basil

¼ cup (30 g) panko bread crumbs

8 slices bread

1 cup (150 g) shredded mozzarella cheese

1 cup (240 g) Red Onion Cranberry Tarragon Jam (page 35)

Preheat the oven to 400°F (200°C, or gas mark 6) and line a baking sheet with parchment paper. In a bowl, use your hands to coat the eggplant in the oil. Sprinkle with salt and spread on the prepared baking sheet. Bake until the eggplant is soft and the edges are a deep golden brown, about 25 minutes. Remove from the oven and set aside to cool.

Meanwhile, spread the nuts on a baking sheet and toast them until they are evenly darker in color, 10 to 15 minutes. Remove from the oven and set aside to cool.

In a food processor, combine the eggplant, walnuts, Parmesan cheese, egg, basil, and bread crumbs. Blend until the mixture just comes together. Shape the eggplant mixture into a square on a baking sheet. Bake for 30 to 40 minutes, or until the exterior has developed a crust and is golden brown. Set aside until it is cool enough to handle. Slice into 4 pieces.

On a work surface, lay out the bread and top each slice with mozzarella cheese. Top 4 slices with ¼ cup (60 g) each of the Red Onion Cranberry Tarragon Jam and top the other 4 slices of bread with a slice of eggplant-walnut loaf. Transfer to a baking sheet and bake until the cheese has melted and the bread is toasted, 5 to 7 minutes. Place the jam-covered bread on top of the meatloaf-topped bread to make 4 sandwiches. Enjoy while warm.

FEATURED SUPERFOODS:
Basil, cranberries, eggs, garlic, olive oil, onions, tarragon, walnuts

MUSTARDY PEANUT CHICKEN WITH POLISH CABBAGE SLAW

RECOMMENDED BREAD: Buckwheat Caraway Beet Bread,
Buttermilk Whole Wheat Bread, sub rolls

YIELD: 4 sandwiches

Both my husband and I have Polish roots and we tend to draw on a lot of Eastern European flavors for inspiration. This cabbage slaw is actually my husband's recipe, and I love how happy he gets whenever we make it, which is pretty often in the colder months. If you make it with the beet bread, the results are a true Polish treat.

4 cups (280 g) thinly shredded red cabbage

1 tablespoon (15 ml) extra-virgin olive oil

1 tablespoon (6 g) caraway seeds

1½ teaspoons kosher salt, divided

¼ cup (60 ml) apple cider vinegar

1 Granny Smith apple, cored and thinly sliced

3 cups (450 g) peanuts

4 boneless, skinless chicken breasts

1 cup (120 g) flour

¼ cup (44 g) Dijon mustard

3 eggs

8 slices bread

Preheat the oven to 400°F (200°C, or gas mark 6) and line a baking sheet with parchment paper. In a medium-size pot over medium heat, combine the cabbage, oil, and caraway seeds. Add ½ teaspoon of the salt. Lower the heat to medium-low and cook the cabbage until it starts to wilt, about 15 minutes. Add the vinegar and cook for another 15 to 20 minutes, until the cabbage is wilted. Stir in the apple. Remove from heat and set aside.

Using a food processor or blender, crush the peanuts until they are very fine. Set aside.

Wrap a chicken breast loosely in plastic wrap and using either a meat mallet or the bottom of a heavy skillet, pound the chicken until it is evenly thin. In a shallow bowl, place the flour. In a second shallow bowl, combine the mustard and eggs. In a third shallow bowl, combine the crushed peanuts with the remaining 1 teaspoon salt. Dredge the chicken in the flour, shaking to remove any excess. Dredge it in the egg-mustard mixture and then the peanut mixture. Lay on the prepared baking sheet and repeat this process for each of the chicken breasts. Bake for 10 to 15 minutes, or until cooked through and registering an internal temperature of 165°F (74°C).

To assemble, lay out the bread and place a chicken breast on 4 of the slices. Top with even amounts of cabbage slaw. Finish with the other slices of bread.

FEATURED SUPERFOODS:
Apples, cabbage, eggs, olive oil, peanuts

TURKEY AND BLACK BEAN CHORIZO PATTY SANDWICH

RECOMMENDED BREAD: Cornmeal Texas Toast, Buttermilk Whole Wheat Bread, Cayenne Maple Sweet Potato Biscuits

YIELD: 4 sandwiches

We make this quick version of turkey chorizo often when we have leftover ground meat. It's not authentic, but it hits all of those smoky, spicy notes that are perfect for when you want something fast, but still want it to be special. This tends to be our late night go-to when we've been busy all day and haven't had much time to stop and eat. It's packed with protein from the turkey, beans, and yogurt sauce. I like to make the patties on the small side, almost to the point of being slider-size. Also, they freeze beautifully.

1 teaspoon extra-virgin olive oil

1 teaspoon minced garlic

Kosher salt

½ pound (227 g) ground turkey

1 cup (250 g) canned black beans, rinsed and drained

1 teaspoon ground cumin

¼ teaspoon ground coriander

1¼ teaspoons smoked paprika

1 tablespoon (18 g) tomato paste

Generous pinch of cayenne, or to taste

½ cup (120 g) Greek yogurt

1 teaspoon lime zest

1 tablespoon (15 ml) fresh lime juice

8 slices bread

¼ cup (4 g) chopped cilantro

In a large skillet over medium heat, heat the oil for a minute or two and then add the garlic and a pinch of salt. Sweat the garlic until it softens, about 3 minutes. Remove from the heat and set aside to cool.

In a large bowl, combine the turkey, black beans, cumin, coriander, paprika, tomato paste, cayenne, and salt to taste. Add the garlic and stir with a spoon or your hands. Shape the mixture into 8 miniature patties.

Return the skillet to medium-high heat and add the patties. Cook for about 5 minutes on each side, or until the internal temperature reaches 165°F (74°C). Set aside to rest.

Meanwhile, combine the yogurt, lime zest, and lime juice in a small bowl to make a crema.

To assemble the sandwiches, lay out the bread and top 4 of the slices with 2 patties each. Drizzle the lime crema on top. Finish with a sprinkling of cilantro and top with the other slices of bread.

FEATURED SUPERFOODS:
Beans, cilantro, cumin, garlic, Greek yogurt, limes, olive oil, peppers, tomatoes, turkey

THAI PEANUT CHICKEN SANDWICH WITH MARINATED CUCUMBER

RECOMMENDED BREAD: Sub rolls, Honey Miso Whole Wheat Sesame Buns, burger buns

YIELD: 4 sandwiches

This sandwich is a take on the classic chicken satay with peanut sauce. The richness of the peanut sauce, which also is fantastic blended with rice noodles or a thin vermicelli, is balanced by crunchy marinated cucumbers. I like to eat this sandwich slightly chilled because the cucumbers are extra refreshing, especially if you got a little heavy-handed with the sriracha. This sandwich is ideal for travel and hot summer days.

1 cup (120 g) half-moon slices English cucumber

2¼ teaspoons rice vinegar, divided

1 teaspoon mirin

1 tablespoon (15 ml) extra-virgin olive oil

1½ pounds (680 g) boneless, skinless chicken breasts

1 teaspoon kosher salt

⅔ cup (170 g) smooth peanut butter

½ cup (120 ml) warm water

2 tablespoons (30 ml) soy sauce

½ teaspoon freshly grated ginger

Sriracha sauce, to taste (optional)

4 rolls, sliced in half

¼ cup (4 g) fresh cilantro leaves

Preheat the oven to 375°F (190°C, or gas mark 5). In a medium-size bowl, combine the cucumber with 2 teaspoons of the vinegar and the mirin. Stir to combine and set aside.

Heat the oil in a large ovenproof skillet over medium-high heat for about 2 minutes. Season the chicken with the salt and place in a single layer in the skillet, being careful not to have the chicken too close together. (It won't brown if it's too close.) Sear the chicken on one side, 5 to 7 minutes, and then flip it over and cook for another 5 to 7 minutes. If the internal temperature of the chicken hasn't reached 165°F (74°C), put the skillet into the oven and bake until it's cooked through, 7 to 10 minutes. Set the chicken aside to rest, about 5 minutes. Once it has rested, pull the meat apart with your hands.

Meanwhile, combine the peanut butter, water, soy sauce, ginger, and remaining vinegar in a medium-size bowl. If the sauce is too thick, add more warm water, just be sure to also add a couple of extra splashes of soy sauce. Add the sriracha, if using. Add the pulled chicken to the peanut sauce and toss to combine.

Divide the chicken evenly among each roll. Top with the marinated cucumbers and finish each sandwich by topping with the cilantro.

FEATURED SUPERFOODS:
Cilantro, ginger, olive oil, peanut butter

PORTOBELLO MUSHROOM SANDWICH WITH CRISPY KALE AND ROSEMARY WHITE BEAN SPREAD

RECOMMENDED BREAD: Parmesan Kale Bread, Buttermilk Whole Wheat Bread, burger buns

YIELD: 4 sandwiches

We make the Rosemary White Bean Spread in this recipe often when we have company and it goes over quite well. Rosemary and white beans make a great pair, and the crispy kale supplies a healthy crunch. The trick to making a good, crispy kale is to keep an eye on it in the oven. Once it goes from all green to brown in some spots and is crunchy all over, it's done. Otherwise, it can burn easily.

4 portobello mushroom caps

2 teaspoons extra-virgin olive oil, divided

1 teaspoon salt, divided, plus more to taste

3 cups (210 g) kale, stemmed

1 cup (250 g) white beans, rinsed and drained

½ teaspoon minced garlic

1 teaspoon chopped fresh rosemary

1 teaspoon fresh lemon juice

8 slices bread

Preheat the oven to 400°F (200°C, or gas mark 6) and line a baking sheet with parchment paper. Scrub the mushroom caps thoroughly and using a spoon, scrape out the gills (the brown part underneath the cap). Slice into thin strips. Heat 1 teaspoon of the oil in a large skillet and add the sliced mushrooms. Cook until they soften and brown, 10 to 15 minutes. Add ½ teaspoon of the salt, stir to combine, and remove from the heat.

Wash and dry the kale and spread in a single layer on the prepared baking sheet. Toss with the remaining 1 teaspoon olive oil and ½ teaspoon salt. Bake the kale until it gets very crispy, 10 to 15 minutes. Remove from the oven and set aside.

Meanwhile, add the beans, garlic, rosemary, and lemon juice to a food processor or blender. Try puréeing it first on its own and then, if needed, add water by the ¼ cupful (60 ml) until you've got a nice smooth purée. Add the water gradually to avoid ending up with a watery mess. If you add water, adjust your seasoning, and add more salt and lemon juice.

To assemble the sandwiches, lay out the slices of bread and spread each with the Rosemary White Bean Spread. Divide the mushrooms among 4 slices of bread. Top with the kale and remaining slice of bread.

FEATURED SUPERFOODS:
Beans, garlic, kale, lemons, mushrooms, olive oil, rosemary

SMOKY TURKEY AND KIDNEY BEAN CHILI SANDWICH

RECOMMENDED BREAD: Cornmeal Texas Toast, Buttermilk Whole Wheat Bread, sub rolls

YIELD: 4 sandwiches

We like chili in our house. A lot. And we tend to eat it regularly, especially during football season. Our eyes always manage to be bigger than our stomachs because we always have lots left over. We've taken to making quick sandwiches the next day with the leftover chili, sort of like a Sloppy Joe. This is a fast version of chili that's a little thicker in nature, so it's perfect to spoon onto some bread. (You can make it vegan by leaving out the turkey.) It tends to be a deliciously messy sandwich, so make sure you have the napkins handy!

1 teaspoon extra-virgin olive oil

½ cup (80 g) half-moon slices red onion

¾ cup (120 g) sliced bell pepper

1 teaspoon kosher salt, divided

1 teaspoon garlic

¾ pound (340 g) ground turkey

1 teaspoon ground cumin

½ teaspoon ground coriander

½ teaspoon ancho chili powder

1 teaspoon smoked paprika

1½ cups (270 g) diced tomatoes

1 cup (250 g) kidney beans, rinsed and drained

¼ cup (4 g) roughly chopped cilantro

8 slices bread

In a medium-size pot, heat the oil over medium heat for 1 minute. Add the onion and pepper and ½ teaspoon of the salt. Sweat the vegetables until they soften, 3 to 5 minutes. Add the garlic and heat for another 1 to 2 minutes. Once the garlic has softened a bit, add the turkey along with the cumin, coriander, chili powder, and paprika. Stir the turkey to combine it with the other ingredients and break it up a bit. Add the tomatoes and remaining ½ teaspoon salt. Heat until the turkey is cooked through and the tomatoes have softened just enough to become a little saucy. Add the kidney beans and stir to combine. Just before serving, add the cilantro to the mix.

To assemble, lay out the bread and top 4 of the slices with equal amounts of the chili mixture. Top with the remaining slices of bread.

FEATURED SUPERFOODS:
Beans, cilantro, cumin, garlic, olive oil, onions, peppers, tomatoes, turkey

ORANGE ROAST LAMB SANDWICH WITH CHAI LENTIL HUMMUS

RECOMMENDED BREAD: Spelt and Flaxseed Challah, Buttermilk Whole Wheat Bread

YIELD: 4 sandwiches, about 1½ cups (360 g) hummus

In the wintertime, I drink a lot of chai tea and chai lattes. The varying mix of spices that make up chai—usually a blend of ginger, cardamom, clove, nutmeg, and allspice—is what inspired the spread on this sandwich. As a whole, it's not shy on flavor, and that's why I like it. The combination of mustard and orange pairs well with the lamb, and the Chai Lentil Hummus adds such a depth of spice and complements the lamb beautifully. The recipe for the hummus makes more than you'll need for the sandwiches, so there's extra for dipping or just slathering on toast for a healthy little snack.

SANDWICH

½ cup (88 g) Dijon mustard

1 tablespoon (6 g) orange zest

2 tablespoons (30 g) fresh orange juice

1 teaspoon chopped fresh rosemary

1 teaspoon minced garlic

1½ pounds (680 g) boneless lamb, trimmed of any thick, exterior fat

1 tablespoon (18 g) kosher salt, plus more to taste

8 slices bread

½ cup (120 g) Chai Lentil Hummus (page 123)

1 cup (30 g) fresh baby spinach

½ cup (75 g) crumbled feta cheese

To make the sandwich: Preheat the oven to 350°F (180°C, or gas mark 4). In a small bowl, combine the mustard, orange zest, orange juice, rosemary, and garlic to make a paste. Spread the paste evenly all over the lamb. Sprinkle with 1 tablespoon (18 g) of the salt and place the lamb in a small baking dish with a lid. Add just enough water so that the bottom of the pan is covered with about 1 inch (2.5 cm) of water. Cover the pan and cook the lamb until tender, about 2 hours. (You can leave it in for longer at a lower temperature of 325°F [170°C, or gas mark 3] for about 2½ to 3 hours for even more tender meat.) Take it out halfway through and baste the lamb with its juices. Once the lamb is cooked through, remove from the oven and set aside, leaving it in the pot to stay warm. When ready to use, remove the lamb from the pot and thinly slice.

Spread the hummus evenly on each slice of bread. Layer the spinach on 4 of the slices and top with the feta, sliced lamb, and remaining bread.

HUMMUS

1 cup (192 g) black beluga lentils, rinsed and picked through for any stones

1 teaspoon kosher salt, plus more to taste

2 cups (470 ml) water

2 chai tea bags, preferably decaf

1 teaspoon honey

1 teaspoon garam masala

1 cup (240 g) Greek yogurt

2 tablespoons (30 ml) fresh lemon juice

Black pepper, to taste

To make the hummus: In a small pot, combine the lentils, 1 teaspoon of the salt, and the water. Bring to a boil, add the chai tea bags, and then reduce the heat to low and simmer until the lentils are cooked through, 15 to 20 minutes. Remove and discard the tea bags. Pour the lentils into a food processor or use a potato masher to purée them. Add the honey, garam masala, Greek yogurt, and lemon juice and stir to combine. If the mixture is too thick, add water until you reach the desired consistency. Season to taste with salt and pepper. Refrigerate in an airtight container for up to 1 week.

FEATURED SUPERFOODS:

Garlic, Greek yogurt, honey, lemons, lentils, oranges, rosemary, spinach

OREGANO-ORANGE CRUSHED CHICKPEA SANDWICH

RECOMMENDED BREAD: Sub rolls, burger buns

YIELD: 4 sandwiches

We always keep dried beans of many varieties, sizes, and colors in our pantry. To make them, it's usually best to soak them overnight and then cook them in salted water the next day, just until they are softened. Because this can be time-consuming, we also keep cans of beans on hand. The texture and flavor of canned beans is less robust than the dried variety, but when time is of the essence, they totally work. This sandwich is made from mashing chickpeas until they are smooth but still chunky. The herbs and spices add flavor and, thanks to the turmeric, a sunny yellow hue that is further punctuated by the orange zest and juice.

1 cup (150 g) walnuts

1½ cups (360 g) chickpeas, rinsed and drained

1 teaspoon chopped fresh oregano

½ teaspoon turmeric

1 tablespoon (15 ml) fresh orange juice

1 teaspoon fresh orange zest

Kosher salt, to taste

4 sub rolls, sliced in half

1 cup (30 g) fresh baby spinach

Preheat the oven to 400°F (200°C, or gas mark 6). Spread the walnuts in a single layer on a baking sheet. Bake until the walnuts brown, 10 to 15 minutes. Remove from the oven and set aside to cool.

In a large bowl, combine the chickpeas, oregano, turmeric, orange juice, and orange zest. Season to taste with salt. Using a potato masher or the back of a fork, roughly mash the chickpeas until they are crushed.

Lay out the sub rolls. Divide the chickpea mixture among 4 rolls. Top each with one-fourth of the walnuts, ¼ cup (7.5 g) of the spinach, and the remaining rolls.

FEATURED SUPERFOODS:
Chickpeas, oranges, oregano, spinach, turmeric, walnuts

MIDDLE EASTERN–SPICED HUMMUS SANDWICH

RECOMMENDED BREAD: Sub rolls, Middle Eastern–Spiced Oat Flaxseed Buns, Honey Miso Whole Wheat Sesame Buns

YIELD: 4 sandwiches

Hummus is incredibly versatile, and making your own at home is so simple. This version calls on a blend of Middle Eastern ingredients and pomegranate seeds, which give it texture and snap and also provide a burst of sweet-tart flavor. The main part of this recipe is the hummus, and it makes more than you'll need for four sandwiches, which means a healthy and satisfying snack will be sitting in your fridge, waiting to be enjoyed at another time. That is not a bad thing.

2 tablespoons (40 g) pomegranate molasses

½ teaspoon ground cumin

1½ cups (360 g) canned chickpeas, rinsed and drained

¼ teaspoon sumac

2 tablespoons (30 ml) extra-virgin olive oil

1 teaspoon honey

1 tablespoon (1 g) fresh cilantro

Kosher salt, to taste

½ cup (75 g) pomegranate seeds

1 cup (120 g) sliced cucumber

2 cups (60 g) baby spinach

4 sub rolls, sliced in half

Combine the pomegranate molasses, cumin, chickpeas, sumac, oil, honey, and cilantro in a food processor or blender. Purée until a paste forms. Season to taste with salt and transfer to a bowl. Add the pomegranate seeds and stir to combine.

Lay out the rolls and spread the hummus over each slice. Top 4 of the slices with the cucumber, spinach, and remaining slices.

FEATURED SUPERFOODS:
Chickpeas, cilantro, cumin, honey, olive oil, pomegranates, spinach

EDAMAME FRIED RICE VEGGIE BURGER

RECOMMENDED BREAD: Honey Miso Whole Wheat Sesame Buns, burger buns

YIELD: 4 burgers

This is one of the best uses for leftover rice (either brown or white), and I make these, or some version of them whenever we have some hanging around. The rice has two purposes: to bind the patties together and to give them heartiness. When they are heated in a hot skillet, the exterior also crisps up nicely, giving it a welcome bit of texture. Feel free to make a big batch, because they freeze beautifully. Just make sure you freeze them in a single layer first and on a baking sheet lined with parchment or wax paper. Once they are frozen solid, they can be stacked or conveniently put into a large plastic container.

⅓ cup (55 g) cooked brown or white rice

1 cup (150 g) shelled edamame

1 teaspoon sesame oil

2 teaspoons soy sauce

1 tablespoon (1 g) chopped cilantro

1 tablespoon (6 g) chopped scallion

1 egg

2 teaspoons cornstarch

1 teaspoon grated fresh ginger

½ cup (55 g) shredded carrot

½ cup (75 g) peas

1 tablespoon (15 ml) vegetable oil

4 buns, sliced in half

4 tablespoons (60 g) hoisin sauce

In a food processor, combine the rice, edamame, sesame oil, soy sauce, cilantro, scallion, egg, cornstarch, and ginger. Pulse until the mixture comes together. (Be careful not to process too much or you'll just end up with mush.) Transfer the mixture to a bowl and add the carrot and peas. Combine with a spoon or rubber spatula.

Heat the vegetable oil in a large nonstick skillet over medium-high heat. Divide the rice mixture into 4 equal parts. Shape them into patties with your hands and place in the hot oil. Let the patties cook until they start to brown, 5 to 7 minutes. Flip them over and cook for another 5 to 7 minutes, or until golden brown.

Spread each bun with 1 tablespoon (15 g) of the hoisin sauce. Place a patty in each bun.

FEATURED SUPERFOODS:
Brown rice, carrots, cilantro, edamame, eggs, ginger, sesame oil

BOSTON BAKED BEAN
HUMMUS GRILLED CHEESE

RECOMMENDED BREAD: Buttermilk Whole Wheat Bread

YIELD: 4 sandwiches

This recipe might sound a little odd, but once it's put together it tastes like a barbecue rolled up into a sandwich, and that's a very good thing. To enhance that smoky, barbecue taste, I use smoked Gouda, but really any smoked cheese works well. Another perk of this sandwich? It's named after one of the best cities that I know.

4 slices bacon, diced

½ cup (80 g) diced onion

1 tablespoon (10 g) minced garlic

2 cups (500 g) kidney beans, rinsed and drained

¼ cup (65 g) tomato paste

1 teaspoon Worcestershire sauce

2 tablespoons (22 g) Dijon mustard

1 tablespoon (15 ml) maple syrup

3 tablespoons (60 g) molasses

Kosher salt, to taste

Cayenne pepper, to taste (optional)

½ cup (120 ml) water

8 slices bread

4 slices smoked Gouda

Cook the bacon in a medium-size pot over medium heat until crispy. Remove from the pot and set aside. Leave enough bacon fat to coat the bottom of the pan. Heat the bacon fat over medium heat and add the onion, cooking just until it softens, 5 to 7 minutes. Add the garlic and heat for another minute or so. Add the kidney beans, tomato paste, Worcestershire sauce, Dijon mustard, maple syrup, and molasses. Season with salt, about ½ teaspoon to get things started, and then to taste. Sprinkle in the cayenne, if using. Add the water and simmer over medium-low heat for 10 to 20 minutes, just until the liquid thickens and reduces a bit, allowing the flavors to concentrate. Check for seasoning and the desired level of sweetness and heat. (What you're going for is a nice balance of sweet from the molasses and maple syrup, the tang of the mustard and tomato, and the heat of the cayenne.) Add the crumbled bacon back to the pot and allow the whole thing to cool, just until it's safe enough to handle. Add the mixture to a processor or blender and, if needed, add water by the ¼ cupful (60 ml) and stream it in slowly while you process or blend, adding just enough until you reach the desired consistency, which should be a tad thicker than hummus.

Lay out the bread and top 4 slices with a healthy spread of the Boston Baked Bean Hummus. Top each with 1 slice of cheese and the other slice of bread. Warm a large nonstick skillet over medium heat and add the sandwiches to the skillet. Heat for 3 to 5 minutes on each side, or just until the bread is toasted and the cheese is melted. Let cool for a minute or two before enjoying. Save the rest of the hummus for another use.

FEATURED SUPERFOODS:
Beans, garlic, onions, tomato

SWEET POTATO SANDWICH WITH SPROUTED LENTIL AND CRANBERRY SALSA

RECOMMENDED BREAD: Pita bread, Buttermilk Whole Wheat Bread, Cornmeal Texas Toast, Cayenne Maple Sweet Potato Biscuits

YIELD: 4 sandwiches

Sprouted lentils, or any sprouted beans or seeds for that matter, supply an extra dose of nutrients and as a bonus, have a pleasant little snap to them and an added punch of freshness. In this sandwich, they are a key component in this salsa. Sprouted lentils can either be found in health food stores or you can sprout your own by soaking them in water and letting them sprout.

3 cups (330 g) ¼-inch (6 mm) rounds sweet potato

1 teaspoon extra-virgin olive oil

1 teaspoon kosher salt

½ cup (75 g) dried cranberries

1 cup (235 ml) hot water

¼ cup (35 g) pumpkin seeds

¼ cup (35 g) sprouted lentils (or other sprouted grain, bean, or vegetable)

4 pieces pita bread

2 tablespoons (22 g) Dijon mustard

Preheat the oven to 400°F (200°C, or gas mark 6) and line a baking sheet with parchment paper. Spread the sweet potatoes on the baking sheet, drizzle with the oil, and season with the salt. Roast until the sweet potatoes are soft and just beginning to brown, 20 to 25 minutes.

Meanwhile, hydrate the cranberries in the water until plump, 3 to 5 minutes. Toast the pumpkin seeds in a small nonstick skillet over medium-low heat, until fragrant and light brown, 4 to 6 minutes. In a small bowl, mix the cranberries, pumpkin seeds, and sprouted lentils, stirring to combine.

Heat the pita bread in the oven just until warmed, 3 to 5 minutes. Cut the pita in half vertically, then spread each piece with the mustard. Top with the roasted sweet potatoes and the cranberry lentil mixture.

FEATURED SUPERFOODS:
Cranberries, lentils, olive oil, pumpkin seeds, sweet potatoes

ANCHO BLACK BEAN BURGER

RECOMMENDED BREAD: Cornmeal Texas Toast, burger buns

YIELD: 4 burgers

If you haven't caught on by now, I love making and eating veggie burgers or patties, as I sometimes call them. They keep so well in the freezer for a convenient meal. This is my standby veggie burger recipe and the one I tend to make most regularly. It's got a great spice, and the brown rice offers nutrients and also gives it shape and texture.

½ cup (80 g) cooked brown rice

1½ cups (375 g) black beans, rinsed and drained

¼ cup (4 g) chopped cilantro

1 teaspoon ground cumin

¾ teaspoon ancho chili powder

Kosher salt, to taste

Black pepper, to taste

1 teaspoon extra-virgin olive oil

½ cup (120 g) Tomatillo Yogurt Sauce (page 41)

4 buns, sliced in half

Preheat the oven to 400°F (200°C, or gas mark 6). In a food processor, purée the rice, beans, cilantro, cumin, ancho, and salt and pepper to taste, until smooth. Line a baking sheet with parchment paper and drizzle with the olive oil. Form the mixture into patties, to make 4 evenly sized portions. Place on the baking sheet and bake until golden brown and crispy on the outside, 12 to 15 minutes, flipping halfway through if necessary.

When ready to serve, spread a little of the yogurt sauce on each bun and top with a black bean patty.

FEATURED SUPERFOODS:
Beans, brown rice, cilantro, cumin, Greek yogurt, limes, olive oil

Chapter 7

SUPERFOOD SPOTLIGHT:
Protein

ITALIAN SARDINE SALAD SANDWICH

RECOMMENDED BREAD: Parmesan Kale Bread,
Spelt and Flaxseed Challah, sub rolls

YIELD: 4 sandwiches

Sardines are not known for being the most popular at the party (poor guys), but this Italian salad just may make you a believer. And if not, then at least you had a serving of some powerful nutrients while giving this sandwich a try. If you already love sardines, then this recipe is great to have in your back pocket. Because sardines are usually bought in cans, you can keep them in your pantry until you're ready to use them.

2 (3.75-ounce, or 105 g) cans sardines

2 teaspoons fresh lemon juice

½ cup (75 g) chopped cherry tomatoes

2 tablespoons (5 g) chopped fresh basil

1 tablespoon (2.5 g) chopped fresh parsley

8 slices bread

½ cup (120 g) Basil-Avocado "Mayo" (page 42)

1 cup (30 g) chopped watercress

Drain the sardines of any oil and add them to a medium-size bowl. Add the lemon juice, tomatoes, basil, and parsley. Combine with a fork, mashing all of the ingredients together.

To assemble the sandwiches, lay out the bread and spread even amounts of the Basil-Avocado "Mayo" on each piece. Top 4 slices of bread with the watercress, the sardine mixture, and the remaining slices of bread.

FEATURED SUPERFOODS:
Avocados, basil, lemons, limes, parsley, sardines, tomatoes, watercress

SPANISH TORTILLA SANDWICH

RECOMMENDED BREAD: Spelt and Flaxseed Challah, Buttermilk Whole Wheat Bread

YIELD: 4 sandwiches

Spain is one of my favorite countries that I've visited, especially because of the food. A Spanish tortilla is similar to an Italian frittata and is classically made from eggs, thinly sliced potatoes, good olive oil, and salt, and I ate it a lot while traveling there. It is very simple in preparation and incredibly satisfying, especially when sandwiched between two slices of bread and topped with the Smoky and Spicy Red Pepper Pesto. It's a great way to start (or end) the day.

1 tablespoon (15 ml) extra-virgin olive oil

1½ cups (165 g) thinly sliced Yukon gold potatoes (about 2 small potatoes)

1 teaspoon kosher salt, plus more to taste

4 large eggs

8 slices bread, toasted

¾ cup (180 g) Smoky and Spicy Red Pepper Pesto (page 38)

Preheat the oven to 350°F (180°C, or gas mark 4). In a small, ovenproof skillet, heat the oil over medium-high heat. Add the potato slices and coat them in the oil. Sprinkle the salt on top. Cook the potato slices, turning them frequently, until they are golden brown and cooked through, 15 to 20 minutes. Remove the skillet from the heat and allow to cool.

While the skillet is cooling, whisk the eggs together with a pinch of salt. Arrange the potato in a single layer on the bottom of the skillet and add the eggs. Turn the heat onto medium-low and, using a rubber spatula, gently run the rubber spatula around the skillet and let the bottom set. Gently push the spatula under the eggs. (This will force uncooked eggs to the bottom, which will help it cook evenly.) Place the skillet in the oven to cook the rest, 5 to 7 minutes, or just until the eggs have set. Run the rubber spatula around the outside of the tortilla to loosen it from the skillet. Transfer to a cutting board, sprinkle with salt, and cut into 4 equal pieces.

Place a piece of tortilla onto 4 slices of bread, generously spread the other 4 slices with the Smoky and Spicy Red Pepper Pesto, and place on top.

FEATURED SUPERFOODS:

Chives, cilantro, eggs, hazelnuts, lemons, olive oil, pecans, peppers

QUINOA-CRUSTED EGGPLANT PARMESAN SUB

RECOMMENDED BREAD: Sub rolls, Parmesan Kale Bread,
Buttermilk Whole Wheat Bread, burger buns

YIELD: 4 subs

A play on a classic eggplant Parmesan sub, the eggplant in this dish is coated with cooked quinoa, which gives it a great crunch. Fresh mozzarella cheese gets melted on top, because, after all, what's an eggplant sandwich without melty cheese? A simple salsa is made from tomatoes, basil, and a splash of balsamic vinegar to add a note of brightness to the sandwich.

1 cup (173 g) quinoa, rinsed and drained

2 cups (470 ml) water

1 teaspoon kosher salt

1 large eggplant

1½ cups (180 g) all-purpose flour

2 eggs

¼ pound (112 g) fresh mozzarella cheese

2 cups (300 g) grape tomatoes, halved

¼ cup (10 g) chopped basil

2 tablespoons (30 ml) balsamic vinegar

4 sub rolls, sliced in half

Preheat the oven to 425°F (220°C, or gas mark 7). Combine the quinoa, water, and salt in a medium-size pot. Bring to a boil and then turn to low, simmering until the quinoa has puffed up and the water has absorbed, about 20 minutes. Transfer the quinoa to a bowl and refrigerate until cool.

While the quinoa is cooking, slice the eggplant into 1-inch (2.5 cm) thick rounds. Spread the flour in a shallow bowl and crack the eggs into a second shallow bowl and beat with a whisk. Add the cooled quinoa to a third shallow dish. Take each eggplant round and dredge it in the flour, shaking off any excess. Dunk the floured eggplant into the egg, and then finally use your fingers to crust the eggplant slice with quinoa. Repeat for each slice of eggplant and lay them on the prepared baking sheet. Bake for about 30 minutes, flipping each one over halfway through, until the eggplant is soft and cooked through and the quinoa has formed a crunchy crust. Top each slice with just enough cheese to cover the top. Set the oven to broil and broil the eggplant until the cheese gets bubbly and starts to develop brown spots. Remove from the heat and set aside.

In a small bowl, combine the tomatoes, basil, and vinegar. To assemble the sandwiches, lay out the sub rolls and divide up the eggplant slices among them. Top with the tomato-basil mixture.

FEATURED SUPERFOODS:
Basil, eggs, quinoa, tomatoes

CUMIN-RUBBED SALMON SANDWICH WITH ROASTED TOMATO GARLIC SALSA

RECOMMENDED BREAD: Cornmeal Texas Toast, sub rolls, burger buns, Buttermilk Whole Wheat Bread

YIELD: 4 sandwiches

The salsa that the salmon in this recipe gets topped with is my go-to salsa recipe. It's very easy to make; just roast the vegetables and then puree until they come together. In the summer, I like to make it in big batches to have on hand. It's great for tortilla chips and other dippable items—and also on sandwiches!

4 medium-size plum tomatoes, halved

1 clove garlic, unpeeled

½ cup (80 g) large-diced onion

1 small jalapeño pepper (optional)

1½ teaspoons lime zest

1 tablespoon (15 ml) lime juice

½ cup (8 g) fresh cilantro

Kosher salt, to taste

1½ pounds (680 g) salmon

1 tablespoon (7 g) ground cumin

8 slices bread

Preheat the oven to 400°F (200°C, or gas mark 6). Line 2 baking sheets with parchment paper. Place the tomatoes, garlic, onion, and jalapeño on one of the prepared sheets. Roast until the onion gets very soft and the tomatoes start to shrink, 25 to 30 minutes. The garlic may take less time so just keep an eye on it and remove it from the oven once it gets soft. You may need to remove some of the items from the baking sheet early if you find that they are roasting faster than the others. Once all of the vegetables are roasted, remove from the oven and set aside to cool just enough to be handled comfortably. Peel the garlic skin and add the soft flesh and the rest of the vegetables to a blender or food processor. Add the lime zest, lime juice, and cilantro. Purée or pulse for a couple of seconds, just until everything comes together but before it becomes a unified purée. Season to taste with salt and add more lime if needed. Set aside until ready to use.

Rub the salmon with the cumin and season with salt. Cut into 4 equal pieces. Roast the salmon on the second prepared baking sheet, skin side down, for about 15 minutes, or until the desired doneness. Remove from the oven and remove and discard the skin.

To assemble the sandwiches, lay out the bread and top 4 slices with a piece of salmon. Top with the salsa and the remaining bread.

FEATURED SUPERFOODS:
Cilantro, cumin, garlic, limes, onions, peppers, salmon, tomatoes

OYSTER "ROCKEFELLER" SANDWICH WITH SALSA VERDE

RECOMMENDED BREAD: Sub rolls, Cornmeal Texas Toast

YIELD: 4 sandwiches

The legend of Oysters Rockefeller goes like this: Antoine, a frustrated restaurateur from New York, leaves for New Orleans to start over. He starts a family-run restaurant where his son creates an oyster dish that is so intensely rich that he names it after the richest man in the country at the time, John D. Rockefeller. The dish is a hit, but no one in the family shares the recipe. They claim that no one has ever successfully duplicated the dish, though many have tried. This sandwich is a tribute to the legend with a few superfood additions, naturally.

1 cup (30 g) loosely packed watercress

¾ cup (45 g) finely chopped fresh parsley, divided

1 tablespoon (6 g) lemon zest

1 teaspoon fresh thyme

Kosher salt

Black pepper

¼ cup (15 g) panko bread crumbs

¼ cup plus 2 tablespoons (90 ml) lemon juice, divided

8 fresh oysters, scrubbed well, shucked, shells reserved

3 tablespoons (24 g) capers

2 cloves garlic, roughly chopped

3 tablespoons (45 ml) olive oil

4 sub rolls, sliced in half

Preheat the oven to 400°F (200°C, or gas mark 6). Finely chop the watercress. Add it and ¼ cup (15 g) of the parsley, the lemon zest, thyme, and a pinch of salt and pepper to a small bowl. Add the bread crumbs and 2 tablespoons (30 ml) of the lemon juice. Stir to combine.

Place each oyster back in a shell and top with the herb–bread crumb mixture. Place on a baking sheet and bake until the bread crumbs have browned, 8 to 10 minutes. Cool slightly, and then slip the oysters (with the topping) out of the shells.

Meanwhile, in a blender, combine the remaining ½ cup (30 g) parsley, remaining ¼ cup (60 ml) lemon juice, the capers, garlic, oil, and a pinch of salt and pepper. Blend until almost smooth, leaving a little texture if desired. Spread the mixture on the sub rolls and top each with 2 oysters.

FEATURED SUPERFOODS:
Garlic, lemons, olive oil, oysters, parsley, watercress

TARRAGON SALMON CAKE WITH AVOCADO, ORANGE, AND WALNUT SALSA

RECOMMENDED BREAD: Sub rolls, burger buns,
Middle Eastern–Spiced Oat Flaxseed Buns

YIELD: 4 sandwiches

Salmon and chicken are the two proteins that are most often requested by our clients, so to keep things fresh and exciting, we create lots (and lots) of versions. Salmon cakes are a staple of ours because they are versatile, leaving lots of room for creativity. This recipe pairs a salmon cake that has a hint of tarragon with a salsa that gives this sandwich a welcome freshness, not to mention a pop of vibrant color.

1 orange, peeled, segmented, and diced

¼ cup (35 g) crushed walnuts

1 avocado, peeled, pitted, and diced

¼ cup (4 g) roughly chopped cilantro

1 pound (474 g) salmon, skin removed

1 teaspoon orange zest

1 tablespoon (11 g) Dijon mustard

2 large eggs

2 tablespoons (8 g) chopped tarragon

½ cup (120 g) Greek yogurt

⅔ cup (35 g) panko bread crumbs

½ teaspoon kosher salt

4 sub rolls or burger buns, sliced in half

Preheat the oven to 400°F (200°C, or gas mark 6). Line a baking sheet with parchment paper. Combine the oranges, walnuts, avocado, and cilantro in a bowl. Stir gently to combine. Set aside until ready to use.

To make the salmon cakes, cut the salmon into small, ½-inch (1.3 cm) dice and place in a bowl. Add the orange zest, mustard, eggs, tarragon, Greek yogurt, bread crumbs, and salt. Blend the salmon mixture with your hands and chill in the refrigerator for 30 minutes. Divide into 4 burger-size cakes and place on the prepared baking sheet. Bake for 20 to 30 minutes, or until the salmon is cooked through and the outside starts to develop a light brown crust.

Place a salmon cake on each sub roll and top with the Orange and Walnut Salsa.

FEATURED SUPERFOODS:
Avocados, cilantro, eggs, Greek yogurt, oranges, salmon, tarragon, walnuts

POLISH TUKEY BURGER WITH HORSERADISH MIZERIA

RECOMMENDED BREAD: Buckwheat Caraway Beet Bread,
Semolina Quinoa Focaccia, burger buns, sub rolls

YIELD: 4 sandwiches

Mizeria is a classic Polish cucumber salad that supposedly gets its name because it was popular among poor, or "miserable," people. If you've ever had Greek tzatziki, it's similar to that but with a bit more sweetness and a stronger tang. It's the perfect topping for this turkey burger of classic Polish flavors such as dill, caraway, and garlic. When it's paired with Buckwheat Caraway Beet Bread, it becomes something truly special.

1 cup (120 g) thinly sliced English cucumber

½ cup (120 g) Greek yogurt

3 tablespoons (12 g) chopped fresh dill, divided

1 tablespoon (15 ml) champagne vinegar

Pinch of sugar

1 teaspoon kosher salt

1½ pounds (680 g) ground turkey

2 teaspoons caraway seeds

½ teaspoon minced garlic

1 tablespoon (15 ml) extra-virgin olive oil

8 slices bread

In a medium-size bowl, combine the cucumbers, Greek yogurt, and 2 tablespoons (8 g) of the dill. Stir in the vinegar and sugar. Set aside until ready to use.

Preheat the oven to 375°F (190°C, or gas mark 5). To make the burgers, combine the salt, turkey, caraway seeds, garlic, and remaining 1 tablespoon (4 g) dill. Blend with your hands just until everything comes together. Divide the mixture up into 4 patties. Make an indent in the center of each patty with your thumb. (This will prevent the burgers from puffing up in the center.)

Warm the oil in a large ovenproof skillet over medium-high heat. Add the burgers and sear until golden brown, 5 to 7 minutes. If they aren't cooked through, transfer the skillet to the oven and cook until the internal temperature reaches 165°F (74°C). Set aside to rest.

To assemble the sandwiches, lay out the bread and top 4 slices with a patty. Top with the mizeria and the other slices of bread.

FEATURED SUPERFOODS:
Dill, garlic, Greek yogurt, olive oil, turkey

KITCHEN SINK SCRAMBLED EGG SANDWICH

RECOMMENDED BREAD: Parmesan Kale Bread,
Middle Eastern–Spiced Oat Flaxseed Buns, English muffins

YIELD: 4 sandwiches

One morning, I threw together a breakfast sandwich using a bunch of ingredients that I had left over from developing recipes. I hadn't planned on putting it in the book, but it was just too good not to. I wrote down exactly what was in it, but the truth is that any scraps and bits of vegetables, meat, and cheese will work, and throwing it together couldn't be easier.

1 cup (120 g) peeled and diced sweet potato

2 teaspoons extra-virgin olive oil

½ teaspoon kosher salt, divided

4 slices Canadian bacon, diced

½ cup (90 g) diced tomato

1 cup (70 g) roughly chopped kale

2 tablespoons (20 g) minced black garlic

3 eggs

½ cup (60 g) diced smoked mozzarella cheese

8 slices bread

Preheat the oven to 400°F (200°C, or gas mark 6) and line a baking sheet with parchment paper. Spread the sweet potatoes on the prepared baking sheet. Toss with the oil and ¼ teaspoon of the salt. Roast the potatoes until they are soft all the way through, 15 to 20 minutes. Remove from the oven and set aside until ready to use.

In a small, nonstick skillet, add the Canadian bacon and cook for 2 to 3 minutes over medium heat. Add the tomato and kale, stir to combine, and cook for 5 to 7 minutes, until the tomatoes have softened and the kale has cooked down. Add the garlic and sweet potatoes and stir to combine.

In a small bowl, whisk together the eggs and remaining ¼ teaspoon salt. Reduce the heat to medium-low and pour the eggs into the skillet with the vegetable and Canadian bacon mixture. Add the cheese to the skillet. Using a plastic spatula, drag it across the bottom of the skillet and up around the edges until the eggs coagulate.

Lay out the bread and divide up the scrambled egg mixture among 4 of the slices. Top each with a remaining slice of bread.

FEATURED SUPERFOODS:
Black garlic, eggs, kale, olive oil, sweet potatoes, tomatoes

SPICY BLACK GARLIC AND SHIITAKE MUSHROOM EGG SANDWICH

RECOMMENDED BREAD: Honey Miso Whole Wheat Sesame Buns

YIELD: 4 sandwiches

This sandwich is great for both breakfast and dinner because it's so satisfying and easy to throw together. Black garlic can be tricky to find, but it's worth the extra effort to search out this slow-cooked treat because it adds a specific sweetness that is hard to replicate. You can buy it online through various retailers, and it usually comes in bulk. It can be pricy, but I assure you it's worth the splurge. If you're anything like me, you'll be hooked and looking for any excuse to include more black garlic in your cooking. Of course, if you can't find black garlic, you can use regular garlic; just reduce the amount to 1 teaspoon.

1 teaspoon sesame oil

1½ cups (105 g) sliced shiitake mushrooms

Kosher salt, to taste

5 large eggs

1 tablespoon (10 g) minced black garlic

1 teaspoon roughly chopped chives

4 buns, sliced in half

Sriracha, to taste

Heat the oil in a medium-size skillet over medium heat and add the mushrooms. Cook until they have softened and are browned, about 10 minutes. Season with salt to taste, remove from the pan, and set aside.

In a small bowl, mix the eggs with a whisk. Add a generous pinch of salt and pour the eggs into the skillet set over medium-low heat. Add the garlic and chives and use the whisk to get the eggs frothy. Whisk continuously until curds start to form, 3 to 4 minutes. Turn off the heat and return the mushrooms to the skillet. Stir to combine.

To assemble the sandwiches, lay out the buns. Divide the eggs among the buns and top with sriracha to taste.

FEATURED SUPERFOODS:
Black garlic, chives, eggs, mushrooms, sesame oil

MEXICAN QUINOA "MEATBALL" SUB

RECOMMENDED BREAD: Sub rolls

YIELD: 4 subs

This recipe will always have a special place in my heart. I created it during the height of my quinoa obsession. This has been the most popular recipe on my blog, and my personal chef clients request it often. It is perfect for people trying to cut back on their meat intake, and it is so versatile, with endless variations.

1 cup (173 g) quinoa, rinsed and drained

2 cups (470 ml) water

1 teaspoon kosher salt

1 teaspoon ground cumin

½ teaspoon ground coriander

1 large egg

¼ cup (4 g) chopped cilantro

¼ cup (30 g) shredded Cheddar cheese

4 sub rolls, sliced in half

1 cup (240 g) Tomatillo Yogurt Sauce (page 41)

Add the quinoa to a medium-size pot. Stir in the water, salt, cumin, and coriander and bring to a boil over medium-high heat. Reduce the heat to low and simmer until the water is absorbed and the quinoa has puffed up, about 20 minutes. Transfer to a large bowl and refrigerate until chilled, and then stir in the egg, cilantro, and cheese.

Preheat the oven to 425°F (220°C, or gas mark 7) and line a baking sheet with parchment paper. Tightly roll the quinoa into golf ball–size "meatballs" and place on the prepared baking sheet. (Make the quinoa balls as tight as possible, or they may fall apart in the oven, which isn't the end of the world because you can just scoop it up into a sloppier and equally delicious sandwich.) Bake for 20 to 30 minutes, just until the outside starts to brown slightly. Remove from the oven and set aside to chill for a couple of minutes because these suckers are hot!

To assemble the subs, lay out the sub rolls. Divide the "meatballs" among the sub rolls and top with the Tomatillo Yogurt Sauce.

FEATURED SUPERFOODS:
Cilantro, cumin, eggs, Greek yogurt, limes, olive oil, quinoa

BETH'S HERBED CRANBERRY TURKEY SANDWICH

RECOMMENDED BREAD: Semolina Quinoa Focaccia, Buttermilk Whole Wheat Bread, Spelt and Flaxseed Challah

YIELD: 4 sandwiches

When I first set out to write this book, I asked my sister, Beth, what her ideal sandwich would be. She paused for a moment to think this over carefully. "It starts with turkey" (I wonder where she gets that from?) "and then maybe there's a fruity component to it." Her face lit up. "And onions! Somehow in an interesting way." My sister has always had a thing for onions. I think she gets that from my grandfather, who couldn't imagine a meal that didn't involve onions. "Lastly, it must have cheese." Voilà—my sister's ideal sandwich. Turns out she was onto something really great.

1 tablespoon (2.5 g) chopped fresh sage

2 teaspoons chopped fresh rosemary

1 teaspoon lemon zest

1 tablespoon (20 g) honey

1 teaspoon minced garlic

1 tablespoon (15 ml) olive oil

1½ pounds (680 g) turkey breast

Kosher salt

1 Granny Smith apple

½ cup (120 g) Red Onion Cranberry Tarragon Jam (page 35)

8 slices bread

4 slices sharp Cheddar cheese

Preheat the oven to 375°F (190°C, or gas mark 5) and line a baking sheet with parchment paper. In a small bowl, combine the sage, rosemary, lemon zest, honey, garlic, and oil. Stir to combine and make a paste. Rub the mixture all over the turkey and season with salt. Lay the turkey on the prepared baking sheet and roast until it is cooked through and registers an internal temperature of 165°F (74°C), 17 to 20 minutes. Let rest, about 5 minutes, before slicing thinly. Core the apple and cut into thin slices.

To assemble the sandwiches, spread an even amount of the jam on 4 slices of bread. Top with the apple slices, a slice of Cheddar cheese, some of the turkey, and the remaining bread. Place the sandwiches on a baking sheet and bake until the cheese melts and the bread crisps, about 10 minutes.

FEATURED SUPERFOODS:
Apples, cranberries, garlic, honey, lemons, olive oil, rosemary, sage, tarragon, turkey

ROASTED SALMON WITH FENNEL AND "EVERYTHING BAGEL" CREAM CHEESE

RECOMMENDED BREAD: Spelt and Flaxseed Challah, bagels, sub rolls, burger buns

YIELD: 4 sandwiches

Cream cheese isn't just for bagels anymore. It's for salmon, too. The flavors that make up an everything bagel—sesame seeds, poppy seeds, garlic, and onion—are the perfect mix for more than just bagels. In this sandwich, that familiar combination finds a home in the cream cheese, which pairs so well with the salmon. The fennel just gives that little extra push that makes this something truly great.

1½ pounds (680 g) salmon

1 cup (100 g) thinly sliced fennel

1 teaspoon extra-virgin olive oil

1 teaspoon kosher salt

4 ounces (112 g) cream cheese

1 teaspoon poppy seeds

¼ teaspoon garlic powder

¼ teaspoon onion powder

1 teaspoon sesame seeds

8 slices bread

Preheat the oven to 375°F (190°C, or gas mark 5) and line a baking sheet with parchment paper. Cut the salmon into 4 equal pieces and place on one side of the prepared baking sheet. You can leave the skin on if it's still there; I find it's easier to remove once the salmon has been cooked. Place the sliced fennel on the other side of the baking sheet. Pour the oil onto the fennel and salmon. Sprinkle both with the salt and bake in the oven for about 15 minutes, or until the salmon reaches the desired level of doneness. The fennel at this point may be done or still need another 10 minutes or so until it has softened significantly and the edges have started to brown. If this is the case, just remove the salmon and continue cooking the fennel. Remove from the oven and set aside. Once the salmon is cool enough to handle, remove the skin and discard.

Meanwhile, combine the cream cheese, poppy seeds, garlic powder, onion powder, and sesame seeds in a small bowl. Stir to combine.

To assemble the sandwiches, spread equal amounts of cream cheese over each slice of bread. Top 4 of the slices with roasted fennel and then follow each with a piece of salmon. Top with the remaining slice of bread.

FEATURED SUPERFOODS:
Olive oil, salmon, sesame seeds

HERBED TURKEY AND ROASTED GRAPE SANDWICH

RECOMMENDED BREAD: Pita bread, Buttermilk Whole Wheat Bread, Semolina Quinoa Focaccia, Parmesan Kale Bread

YIELD: 4 sandwiches

I couldn't imagine having a sandwich cookbook that didn't include a recipe for a turkey sandwich, especially because I lived on them in college. I've created this one, a little more grown-up and sophisticated than my turkey on rye from my college days, thanks to the roasted grapes, which impart a sweet pop of flavor. Roasting fruits really enhances their natural flavors. The turkey itself is kept simple, seasoned only with salt and pepper and roasted just until it's cooked through and still juicy. It plays really well against the plump, roasted grapes.

1 tablespoon (15 ml) extra-virgin olive oil

1½ pounds (680 g) turkey breast

1 teaspoon kosher salt

¼ teaspoon coarsely ground pepper

2 cups (300 g) seedless red grapes

4 pita bread pockets

2 cups (140 g) mâche or other leafy green

Preheat the oven to 375°F (190°C, or gas mark 5) and line a baking sheet with parchment paper. Heat the oil in a large ovenproof skillet over medium-high heat. Season the turkey breast with the salt and pepper. Add it to the hot oil and sear the outsides, about 7 minutes on each side. Place the skillet in the oven to cook the turkey all the way through, until it registers 165°F (74°C) internally, 10 to 15 more minutes. Remove from the oven and set aside to rest, about 5 minutes, before slicing thinly.

While the turkey is cooking, spread the grapes in a single layer on the prepared baking sheet. Roast the grapes until they start to shrivel slightly, 10 to 15 minutes. Set aside to cool.

To assemble the sandwiches, slice open the pita pockets and stuff the mâche, turkey slices, and grapes into each.

FEATURED SUPERFOODS:
Olive oil, turkey

MONTREAL BREAKFAST SANDWICH

RECOMMENDED BREAD: Montreal bagels, sesame bagels, sub rolls, English muffins

YIELD: 4 sandwiches

My father-in-law loves food with great passion but is not much into cooking—except when it comes to breakfast sandwiches. He'll putter around the kitchen, cook the eggs just so, and shower them with freshly ground black pepper. He'll drape the eggs delicately over the chosen bread and meat and generously apply paper-thin slices of sharp Cheddar cheese. If you happen to witness this all going down, he'll probably get caught up in telling you a story or two. But once it's all assembled, he'll grow silent, sit back, and proudly admire his work. He might even say, "Damn, this looks good." And who can blame him? It does.

12 (½-inch, or 1.3 cm) slices tomato

1 tablespoon plus 1 teaspoon (20 ml) extra-virgin olive oil, divided

1 teaspoon Montreal seasoning, divided

4 Montreal bagels or sesame seed bagels, sliced in half

4 slices sharp Cheddar cheese

4 slices Canadian bacon

4 eggs

Line a baking sheet with parchment paper and place the tomato slices on it. Coat with 1 tablespoon (15 ml) of the oil and sprinkle with ½ teaspoon of the Montreal seasoning. Set the oven to broil and, keeping an eye on them, broil the tomatoes until they brown, shrink in size, and are very soft, 5 to 7 minutes. Remove from the oven and set aside. Switch the oven from broil to bake and set at 400°F (200°C, or gas mark 6).

Top 4 bagel halves with a piece of cheese and top the other 4 halves with a piece of Canadian bacon. Place on a baking sheet and bake until the cheese melts and the bagels are toasted, 5 to 7 minutes. Top the cheese side of each bagel with 3 tomato slices.

While the bagels are toasting, add the remaining 1 teaspoon (5 ml) oil to a large skillet and heat over medium heat. Break the eggs one by one into the skillet, making sure they have enough room to spread out. Season the eggs with the remaining ½ teaspoon Montreal seasoning. Cook for 2 to 3 minutes, just until the whites have set and are no longer translucent. Cover the skillet with a lid and cook for another 2 to 3 minutes, just until the top of the egg is cooked and no longer clear, but the yolk is still giggly. Place an egg on top of each bagel sandwich and join the two halves together. Enjoy while warm.

FEATURED SUPERFOODS:
Eggs, olive oil, sesame seeds, tomatoes

Chapter 8

SUPERFOOD SPOTLIGHT:
Spices, Seeds, and Nuts

CINNAMON-SPICED PORK TENDERLOIN SANDWICH

RECOMMENDED BREAD: Cayenne Maple Sweet Potato Biscuits, Spelt and Flaxseed Challah, Buckwheat Caraway Beet Bread

YIELD: 4 sandwiches

This sandwich makes me want to curl up in the coziest and fuzziest sweater that I can find on that first chilly fall day. It's heavy on the cinnamon, but allspice, cloves, and a touch of maple syrup round things out and add a lot of sweet warmth while the apple gives it a fresh crispness.

1 teaspoon ground cinnamon

¼ teaspoon ground cloves

¼ teaspoon allspice

1 teaspoon kosher salt

1½ pounds (680 g) pork tenderloin

1 tablespoon (15 ml) extra-virgin olive oil

1 tablespoon (15 ml) maple syrup

4 biscuits

4 tablespoons (44 g) grainy mustard

1 Granny Smith apple, cored and thinly sliced

Preheat the oven to 375°F (190°C, or gas mark 5). In a small bowl, combine with your hands or a spoon the cinnamon, cloves, allspice, and salt to make a spice rub. Coat the pork with the spice rub. (I usually find it easiest and best just to roll up my sleeves and use my hands to spread it evenly.)

Heat the oil in a large ovenproof skillet and add the pork. Sear, getting color on the pork, 3 to 4 minutes on each side. Place the skillet in the oven to finish cooking, 10 to 15 minutes, or until the internal temperature of the pork is 145°F (63°C). Remove from the oven. Drizzle the maple syrup evenly over the pork and set aside to rest, about 5 minutes. Slice thinly.

Slice the biscuits in half horizontally. Heat them in the oven for a couple of minutes to warm them. Spread each with 1 tablespoon (11 g) of the mustard. Top the bottoms of the biscuits with the apple slices, pork slices, and the tops of the biscuits.

FEATURED SUPERFOODS:
Apples, cinnamon, olive oil

GREEN TEA CUCUMBER SANDWICH

RECOMMENDED BREAD: Semolina Quinoa Focaccia,
Buttermilk Whole Wheat Bread, Parmesan Kale Bread

YIELD: 4 sandwiches

Back in my office days, I used to bring cucumber sandwiches to work all of the time for several reasons: They are easy to assemble, they travel well with the cucumber maintaining its crunch, and they are satisfying enough to keep you filled up but not too heavy so that you wind up feeling sluggish for the rest of the day.

1 green tea bag (regular or decaf)

4 ounces (112 g) cream cheese

2 teaspoons Meyer lemon zest (or regular lemon zest)

1 tablespoon (4 g) chopped dill

8 slices bread

2 cups (240 g) sliced English cucumber

Using scissors, cut open the tea bag and pour the contents into a small, dry skillet. Warm over medium heat until the tea becomes fragrant, about 3 minutes. Set aside to cool. Combine in a small bowl with the cream cheese, lemon zest, and dill.

Lay out the bread and smear each slice with the green tea–cream cheese mixture. Lay the cucumber slices on top. Top with the other slices of bread.

FEATURED SUPERFOODS:
Dill, green tea, lemons

POTATO FLAXSEED LATKE SANDWICH WITH HORSERADISH YOGURT

RECOMMENDED BREAD: Spelt and Flaxseed Challah, burger buns, sub rolls

YIELD: 4 sandwiches

Some people like to dress latkes with a sour cream mixture while others like to take the sweet route, dusting them with cinnamon and sugar and topping them with applesauce. I love them topped with sour cream or yogurt. I've added some pungent horseradish to the mix, which results in a tangy and slightly spicy and very satisfying combo. Try swapping out the potatoes for other root vegetables, such as sweet potatoes, beets, or turnips.

3 cups (360 g) shredded russet potatoes (about 2 medium potatoes)

¼ cup (40 g) shredded shallot (about 2 large shallots)

¼ cup (24 g) flaxseeds

1 egg

¼ cup (30 g) matzo meal, plus more if needed

1 teaspoon kosher salt

3 tablespoons (45 ml) olive oil

½ cup (120 g) Greek yogurt

2 tablespoons (30 g) prepared horseradish, or to taste

¼ cup (12 g) chopped chives

8 slices bread

Preheat the oven to 375°F (190°C, or gas mark 5). Line a baking sheet with parchment paper. In a large bowl, combine the potatoes, shallot, and flaxseeds. Add the egg, matzo meal, and salt and stir to combine. Once combined, the mixture should be slightly wet but stick together. If it doesn't, add another 2 tablespoons (16 g) matzo meal.

Heat the oil over medium-high heat in a large skillet and drop the mixture into the hot oil by the ¼ cupful (60 g). Cook the latkes until they start to get crispy and brown, 3 to 5 minutes. Flip and cook the other side for 3 to 5 minutes, until they brown. Transfer to the prepared baking sheet. You may need to work in batches to avoid crowding the skillet. Bake the latkes for 15 to 20 minutes, or until they are cooked all the way through. Remove from the oven and set aside to cool.

Mix the Greek yogurt with the horseradish and chives in a small bowl. Set aside until ready to use.

Lay out the slices of bread. Divide the horseradish yogurt among each slice. Place one or two latkes each on 4 slices of bread. Top each with the remaining bread.

FEATURED SUPERFOODS:
Chives, eggs, flaxseeds, Greek yogurt, olive oil

MOM'S TURKEY OAT MEATBALL SUB

RECOMMENDED BREAD: Sub rolls

YIELD: 4 subs

If you ever bring up the subject of meatballs around my mom, she'll instantly light up and excitedly encourage you to guess what the "secret ingredient" is in her meatball recipe. She'd give you one, maybe two, guesses before she'd blurt it out: "Oatmeal!" She prides herself on her meatballs, maybe more than anything else she makes. They're light and slightly sweet, thanks to this "secret ingredient." Even though this recipe is slightly tweaked and swaps out beef for turkey, I think she'll still approve. Just keep the secret safe, okay?

3 cups (450 g) grape tomatoes

2 cloves garlic, skins on

1 tablespoon (15 ml) extra-virgin olive oil

¼ cup (10 g) fresh basil

1½ teaspoons kosher salt, divided, plus more to taste

1 pound (454 g) ground turkey

⅔ cup (55 g) oats

1 egg

1 tablespoon (11 g) Dijon mustard

2 tablespoons (32 g) tomato paste

2 teaspoons Worcestershire sauce

¼ cup (15 g) panko bread crumbs, plus more if needed

4 slices smoked mozzarella cheese

4 sub rolls, sliced in half

Preheat the oven to 400°F (200°C, or gas mark 6). Line a baking sheet with parchment paper. In a medium-size ovenproof skillet, add the tomatoes and garlic and drizzle the oil on top. Transfer to the oven and roast until the tomatoes shrink in size and start to brown and the garlic gets very soft, 20 to 25 minutes. Remove from the oven and set aside to cool. Peel the garlic. Once the tomatoes have cooled enough for handling, add them, the garlic, basil, and ½ teaspoon of the salt to a blender or food processor. Blend until smooth and season to taste with salt. Set aside.

In a big bowl, add the turkey, oats, egg, mustard, tomato paste, Worcestershire sauce, bread crumbs, and remaining 1 teaspoon salt. Using your hands, combine everything just until it comes together. If the mixture is still a little on the wet side, add a little more panko. Using your hands, shape the mixture into meatballs and place on the prepared baking sheet. Bake in the oven until their internal temperature registers 165°F (74°C), 15 to 20 minutes. Remove from the oven and set aside to cool.

To assemble the sandwiches, lay the sub rolls on a baking sheet. Top each bottom piece with 3 or 4 meatballs. Top with a slice of cheese and then divide up the tomato sauce among the sandwiches. Bake the sandwiches just until the cheese melts and the bread is toasted, 3 to 5 minutes.

FEATURED SUPERFOODS:
Basil, eggs, garlic, oats, olive oil, tomatoes, turkey

CHIA-SEEDED TOMATO SANDWICH WITH SMOKED MOZZARELLA AND BASIL-AVOCADO "MAYO"

RECOMMENDED BREAD: Sub rolls, burger buns, Parmesan Kale Bread

YIELD: 4 sandwiches

Here's a little update on one of my favorite sandwich staples: the tomato, basil, and mozzarella sandwich. Fun fact: The first mention of mozzarella cheese was back in 1570, in an Italian cookbook, and the popular trio of tomato, basil, and mozzarella is meant to signify the Italian flag. In this dish, the same colors are still present, but I use smoked mozzarella instead, for its flavor. The tomatoes are crusted in chia seeds, which gives this sandwich a lot of character.

8 (½-inch, 1.3 cm) thick tomato slices

3 tablespoons (33 g) chia seeds

4 sub rolls, sliced in half

¾ cup (180 g) Basil-Avocado "Mayo" (page 42)

1 cup (30 g) fresh baby spinach

4 slices smoked mozzarella cheese (or regular mozzarella cheese)

Lay out the slices of tomato and coat them evenly with chia seeds. Lay out the sub rolls and spread with the Basil-Avocado "Mayo." Add the spinach to each roll, and then layer with the smoked mozzarella and 2 slices of chia seed–dusted tomatoes.

FEATURED SUPERFOODS:
Avocados, basil, chia seeds, limes, spinach, tomatoes

COCOA-ORANGE STEAK SANDWICH

RECOMMENDED BREAD: Sub rolls

YIELD: 4 sandwiches

This sandwich was inspired by my mother-in-law, who is the biggest lover of chocolate I've ever met and quite an expert on the subject as well. She has a collection of chocolates from all over the world to boot. Her hands-down favorite combination is dark chocolate (really, the darker the better) and orange. I surprised her with this sandwich, and she went nuts for it. The bittersweetness of the cocoa is balanced by the freshness of the orange, and it all enhances the steak that it coats. Make this for the chocolate lover in your life.

1½ pounds (680 g) skirt steak

1½ tablespoons (12 g) unsweetened cocoa

1½ tablespoons (9 g) orange zest

1 tablespoon (15 ml) grapeseed oil

1 teaspoon kosher salt

½ cup (120 g) Greek yogurt

2 tablespoons (30 ml) fresh squeezed orange juice

4 sub rolls, sliced in half

1 cup (30 g) mâche or other greens

Trim the steak of visible and large chunks of fat. Cut into thin strips and coat with the cocoa powder and orange zest. Heat the oil in a large skillet over medium-high heat, for about 3 minutes. Sprinkle the steak with the salt. Add the steak to the hot oil and cook for about 3 minutes, flipping and cooking for another 3 minutes or so, until the desired doneness. Remove from the heat and set aside to rest.

Combine the yogurt and orange juice in a small bowl.

To assemble the sandwiches, lay out the sub rolls. Spread with the yogurt sauce and top with the steak and mâche.

FEATURED SUPERFOODS:
Cocoa, Greek yogurt, oranges

CRISPY TOFU AND GINGER PICKLED DAIKON BANH MI

RECOMMENDED BREAD: Sub rolls

YIELD: 4 sandwiches

The banh mi was invented as a result of French occupation in Vietnam, marrying ingredients that are French (baguette, mayo) with items that are classically Vietnamese (cilantro, pickled carrots, and daikon). The banh mi has gained a lot of ground stateside. The fillings vary widely but are commonly some sort of meat (beef, pork, or even deli-style meat), a spread of pâté, herbs, and vegetables, some pickled and some not. This is a vegetarian version that is easy to throw together and great for a meal on the go. It has a refreshing quality, thanks to the pickled vegetables, so it's particularly good in the summer.

½ cup (120 ml) rice vinegar

¼ cup (50 g) sugar

½ cup (120 ml) water

2 slices fresh ginger, peeled and cut into matchsticks

Kosher salt, to taste

1 (6-inch, or 15 cm) piece daikon radish, peeled and cut into matchsticks

½ cup (55 g) shredded carrot

1 (16-ounce, or 454 g) package extra-firm tofu, drained

2 tablespoons (30 ml) grapeseed oil

1 jalapeño pepper

1 English cucumber

½ cup (8 g) fresh cilantro

Sriracha, to taste

4 sub rolls, split in half

In a medium saucepan, combine the vinegar, sugar, water, ginger, and a pinch of salt. Bring to a boil, stirring until the sugar has dissolved. Remove from the heat and chill until cold. Once the liquid has cooled, add the radish and carrot and allow to sit in the pickling liquid for at least 10 minutes. (This can be made up to 2 days ahead of time.)

Cut the tofu into 1-inch (2.5 cm) chunks and drain on paper towels. In a large nonstick skillet, heat the oil over medium-high heat. Add the tofu and cook, in batches if necessary, until golden brown and crispy, 5 to 7 minutes per side, being careful not to flip more than once to ensure crispy tofu. Drain on paper towels to remove excess oil.

Meanwhile, slice the jalapeño (removing the seeds if you want it milder) and cucumber into ½-inch (1.3 cm) slices. Separate the cilantro leaves from the stems, chopping the stems if too large, but keeping the leaves whole.

Build a sandwich by squeezing sriracha to taste on each half of each sub roll. Top with a handful of the pickled ginger, daikon, and carrot, and then add the tofu, a few slices of jalapeño and cucumber, and a sprinkling of cilantro.

FEATURED SUPERFOODS:
Carrots, cilantro, ginger, peppers, tofu

BALSAMIC GOJI BERRY–MARINATED CHICKEN SANDWICH

RECOMMENDED BREAD: Sub rolls, Parmesan Kale Bread, Cornmeal Texas Toast, Spelt and Flaxseed Challah

YIELD: 4 sandwiches

Goji berries, which can be found in most health food stores, usually come dried in little pellets. I like to rehydrate them first in boiling water, which brings them back to life, softens them, and plumps them up. They don't have a very strong taste and are slightly sweet and tangy. When they are combined with balsamic vinegar and then cooked and reduced down to a syrupy liquid, they make a great glaze for proteins and vegetables.

½ cup (75 g) dried goji berries

1 cup (235 ml) balsamic vinegar

1½ pounds (680 g) boneless, skinless chicken breasts

¾ teaspoon kosher salt

1 tablespoon (15 ml) extra-virgin olive oil

1 cup (145 g) blackberries

½ cup (70 g) pumpkin seeds

2 tablespoons (5 g) roughly chopped basil

8 slices bread

1 cup (30 g) arugula

Preheat the oven to 375°F (190°C, or gas mark 5). Put the goji berries into a small bowl and pour in just enough boiling water to cover them. Let sit until they plump up. Drain and discard the water. Combine the vinegar and goji berries in a blender and purée until smooth, about a minute or two. Pour into a small saucepan and bring to a boil over medium-high heat. Be careful of the fumes: While balsamic vinegar reduces, it loses its harshness but produces some pretty potent air. Boil the balsamic mixture until it becomes thick and syrupy, 8 to 10 minutes. Transfer to a bowl and set aside to cool.

Meanwhile, season the chicken with the salt. Heat the oil in a large ovenproof skillet over medium heat for a minute or two. Add the chicken to the skillet and sear on one side for 5 to 7 minutes before flipping each breast over and searing on the other side for another 5 to 7 minutes. Pour in the balsamic-goji glaze, turn the chicken to coat, and finish baking the chicken in the oven until it's cooked through and reaches an internal temperature of 165°F (74°C). Set aside to rest for 5 to 7 minutes before slicing into thin strips.

In a medium-size bowl, combine the blackberries, pumpkin seeds, and basil.

To assemble the sandwiches, divide the chicken among 4 slices of bread. Top with the pumpkin seed mixture, a layer of arugula, and the remaining slices of bread.

FEATURED SUPERFOODS:
Arugula, basil, blackberries, goji berries, olive oil, pumpkin seeds

CHIA SEED, PUMPKIN, APPLE, AND TOASTED PECAN WAFFLE SANDWICH

RECOMMENDED BREAD: Whole wheat waffles

YIELD: 4 sandwiches

Growing up in New England, it's hard not to fall madly in love with all things pumpkin. Starting in September, you can come to our house and find something pumpkin-related in the kitchen: bread, cake, leftover pumpkin pancakes, and often a container of pumpkin spread in the fridge, just waiting to be slathered on something. After developing this recipe, we found that the spread in it was also a great dip for graham crackers. The interesting thing about this dip is that chia seeds sort of puff up, as chia seeds do when exposed to something wet, making it rich and thick and packed with all the goodness that chia seeds offer.

2 ounces (56 g) cream cheese, softened

½ cup (130 g) pumpkin purée

2 teaspoons maple syrup

1 tablespoon (6 g) chia seeds

¼ teaspoon grated fresh ginger

Pinch of ground cloves

1 cup (150 g) pecans

1 apple

8 waffles

Preheat the oven to 400°F (200°C, or gas mark 6). In a medium-size bowl, combine the cream cheese, pumpkin, maple syrup, chia seeds, ginger, and cloves with a plastic spatula or spoon. Set aside until ready to use.

Spread the pecans in a single layer on a baking sheet. Toast until golden brown in color, about 10 minutes. Remove from the oven and set aside to cool. Core and slice the apple thinly and set aside.

To assemble the sandwiches, toast the waffles until they are slightly crispy. Spread equal amounts of the pumpkin mixture over every slice. Top 4 of the waffles with the apple slices and pecans. Finish by adding the remaining waffles to make 4 sandwiches.

FEATURED SUPERFOODS:
Apples, chia seeds, ginger, pecans, pumpkin